THE ANNOTATED

U.S. CONSTITUTION

AND DECLARATION

OF INDEPENDENCE

THE ANNOTATED
U.S. CONSTITUTION
AND DECLARATION
OF INDEPENDENCE

Edited by

Jack N. Rakove

The Belknap Press of
Harvard University Press
Cambridge, Massachusetts
and London, England

2009

Library of Congress Cataloging-in-Publication Data

Rakove, Jack N., 1947–

The annotated U.S. Constitution and Declaration of Independence /

edited by Jack N. Rakove.

p. cm.

Includes bibliographical references and index.

ISBN 978-0-674-03606-2 (alk. paper)

1. United States. Constitution.　2. United States. Constitution. 1st–27th
Amendments.　3. United States. Declaration of Independence.
4. Constitutional law—United States.　5. Constitutional history—United States.
I. Rakove, Jack N., 1947–　II. United States. Declaration of Independence.
III. United States. Constitution.　IV. United States. Constitution.
1st–27th Amendments.　V. Title: Annotated United States
Constitution and Declaration of Independence.

KF4527.A56 2009

342.7302—dc22

200902

To my grandparents of blessed memory

Jacob & Rose Rakove

Louis & Nellie Bloom

who, by "making an election of government, more than
of air, soil, or climate, for themselves or their children,"
did secure the blessings of liberty for their posterity.

Contents

Illustrations

A Note to the Reader

The very idea of preparing a concise annotated edition of the Declaration of Independence and the Constitution is almost a contradiction in terms. Both documents have a rich and complicated history that covers both their origins and their subsequent interpretation. To do justice to this richness and complexity in a volume of this size is so obviously impossible that the annotator has no choice but to impose a strong and highly selective voice on the individual entries that accompany the text. In finding that voice, I have tried to combine and balance the historian's natural fascination with the origins of clauses with the modern legal commentator's and concerned citizen's interest in their evolving interpretation. The result will probably satisfy neither historians nor constitutional lawyers, but hopefully it will engage the lay readers and students for whom these annotations have really been prepared.

To keep the commentary on the Constitution as accessible as possible, I have generally avoided giving every subclause or particular provision its own detached annotation. Limitations of space have prevented me from giving some critical clauses anything more than a prelude to the broader treatment they deserve (the First and Fourteenth Amendments being obvious cases in point). The perspective throughout is that of a historian, and indeed this would be a very different volume if prepared by a legal scholar. The opinions presented (and discriminating readers will note a few) are mine alone, and they are meant to provoke as well as inform.

Introduction

ELEVEN YEARS APART, two sets of delegates met in the assembly room of the Pennsylvania Statehouse in Philadelphia and debated the two great documents that define the American political creed. The first set of delegates were members of the Continental Congress that approved the Declaration of Independence on July 4, 1776. The second were the framers of the Federal Constitution that the great Convention of 1787 proposed to the American people on September 17, 1787. Fifty-six delegates from all thirteen states eventually signed the Declaration, not in one grand gesture on July 4, but only after an "engrossed" version—an official copy in large, clear handwriting—was prepared on parchment and laid before Congress on August 2, 1776. Fifty-five members from twelve states (all but Rhode Island) attended the Convention that gathered in Philadelphia in May 1787. Forty-two were still present on September 17, and all but three earned the title of signer that day. George Washington signed the Constitution as presiding officer. On both documents, the order of the signatures follows a geographic axis from north to south, making New Hampshire the first and Georgia the final delegation to sign. On both documents, too, the signatures begin along the right margin of the final page, and then shift to the left. On the Declaration, Georgia has a stragglylooking column all to itself (perhaps fittingly, since it was the last of the thirteen colonies to join the Continental Congress, and was still very much of a frontier outpost). The tiniest signature on the Constitution belongs to James Madison Jr., the Virginia statesman whom we honor as its leading framer.

Whether oversized like John Hancock's or neat like Madison's, the signatures remind us that these documents were products of a particular historical moment and a distinctive set of historical actors. The Declaration and the Constitution have become texts for the ages, subject to the continuing interpretation and reinterpretation that each generation applies to the legacies of the past. But they were also the products of a revolutionary age and the work of budding statesmen who were deeply aware of the unique opportunity they were seizing. John Adams captured this sentiment well when he closed his 1776 pamphlet *Thoughts on Government* by exulting at having "been sent into life at a time when the greatest lawgivers of antiquity would have wished to

The Constitution was a product of a particular historical moment. The signatures—each with its own "personality"—remind us, however, that it was also the product of a distinctive set of historical actors. Some were well-read in law, history, and political philosophy; all shared the common experience of living through a revolutionary experience in self-government.

live." A decade later Alexander Hamilton struck much the same note in the opening paragraph of *The Federalist,* the great commentary that illuminates the original meaning of the Constitution. "It has been frequently remarked," Hamilton observed, "that it seems to have been reserved to the people of this country, by their conduct and example, to decide the important question, whether societies of men are really capable or not of establishing good government from reflection and choice, or whether they are forever destined to depend for their political constitutions on accident and force." Adams had written as a "lawgiver," a modern incarnation of the great solitary figures of antiquity, akin to Moses at Sinai, Solon in Athens, Lycurgus in Sparta. But Hamilton spoke of the American people as the ultimate sources of their own fundamental law, the sovereigns whose consent could transform the Constitution from a set of proposals into a working frame of government.

Creating that American people was the common project of both documents. What the Declaration was really intended to declare was this plain fact: that a new people were preparing to assume their "separate and equal Station" among the nations of the world, bid political adieu to their British countrymen, and seek the political recognition to which "the Laws of Nature and of Nature's God entitle them." The newly independent Americans were now free to exercise their natural right to form a new government. For

Thomas Jefferson the creation of such governments had become so much "the whole object of the present controversy" that he yearned to be back in Williamsburg, working on a constitution for Virginia, rather than stuck in Philadelphia drafting the Declaration. When James Madison was laying his plans for the Federal Convention in 1787, he insisted that "a ratification" of whatever government it produced "must be obtained from the people, and not merely from the ordinary authority of the legislatures." The American people whose nationhood the Declaration first proclaimed thus became a people whose chief source of identity was the national Constitution the lawgivers of 1787 asked them to ratify.

Yet in calling this sovereign people into existence, the authors of the Declaration and the Constitution uneasily confronted one morally embarrassing challenge. In 1776 slavery was legal in all the new states, but the vast majority of African and African American slaves were concentrated in the plantation states, from Maryland south to the frontier outpost of Georgia. Were these hundreds of thousands of slaves who constituted this exploited labor force capable of becoming part of this new American people? In a fiery passage of the Declaration, Jefferson tried to finesse this problem by blaming the British monarchy for imposing the institution of slavery on unwilling American colonists. Congress deleted this entire passage, not only because many southern delegates were committed to slavery, but also because the delegates knew that many colonists were all too happy to draw their own prosperity from the sweat of other brows. Eleven years later the Federal Convention faced a similar problem. How could slaves be counted for purposes of representation when they could never be regarded as citizens in any conceivable sense of the term? To be a slave was to lack all legal rights—to be neither citizen nor subject, but simply an involuntary object of laws imposed on you and your descendants. The framers' solution—to call slaves "other persons" and count each of them as three-fifths of a free person for purposes of allocating representation among the states—was a mark of the moral embarrassment that later led abolitionists like William Lloyd Garrison to denounce the Constitution of 1787 as "a covenant with death."

That Constitution, in a sense, nearly died with the election of Abraham Lincoln to the presidency in 1860 and the ensuing secession crisis of 1861. But it was revived with the three Reconstruction amendments that freed the slaves, affirmed a new version of equal citizenship, and prohibited (at least in principle) "race, color, or previous condition of servitude" from being used to deny the right to vote. The new constitutional vision of the 1860s reflected principles that many Americans had come to ascribe to the Declaration of Independence well *after* its adoption. The equality Americans claimed in 1776 was the right to become a nation like other nations. But in the decades after independence, Americans began reading the Declaration's ringing affirmation that "all men are created equal" in different terms. Now it challenged the hierarchies of social class and legal status, race and gender, that the congressional delegates of 1776 could still take for granted. A vision of equality *among* peoples was giving way to one of equality *within* a people. That was how Lincoln restated the founding proposition that "all men are created equal" in the Gettysburg Address of 1863—a less formal and official document than the texts reprinted in this volume, but one that helped to complete the vision of peoplehood that Jefferson had first articulated four score and seven years earlier.

The adoption of the Declaration climaxed a decade of political agitation and constitutional controversy that began when Parliament approved the Stamp Act of 1765. Until 1775, the central issue in dispute between Britain and its provinces was whether the American colonists were subject to the legislative jurisdiction of Parliament, and, if so, whether that jurisdiction operated "in all cases whatsoever" (as Parliament asserted it did, in the Declaratory Act of 1766), or was limited to a specific class of legislation, particularly the Navigation Acts that regulated the flow of commerce throughout the empire. When the colonists spoke of independence at all, they meant independence from Parliament, not the British crown. In their view, the crown was the proper link between the colonies and the empire, and their own legislative assemblies were to be treated as nearly equivalent to Parliament.

The coming of the American Revolution was *not* a story of one grievance relentlessly piling upon another until something snapped and the colonists decided that national independence was their only recourse. After each crisis, most colonists hoped that the empire would regain its senses, recognize that they were loyal subjects, and allow the colonies to remain the largely autonomous communities they had always been. But in the winter of 1773–1774, one crisis spun out of control, and independence from the entire empire soon became the real possibility Americans had to face.

That crisis was sparked by the Boston Tea Party of 1773. That year Parliament passed the Tea Act, giving the powerful but nearly bankrupt East India Company a monopoly over the sale of legally imported tea in America. Tea was the one item that still carried the duties on selected imports levied by the Townshend Act of 1767, repealed three years later. When tea ships began arriving in the fall of 1773, colonial protests convinced their captains and local officials that the safest course was to sail home to Britain, with cargoes intact. But in Boston, Governor Thomas Hutchinson—a fifth-generation son of New England, but a royal appointee and loyal servant of the empire—refused to permit the ships to

Americans throwing the Cargoes of the Tea Ships into the River, at Boſton

This British engraving, from W. D. Cooper's *History of North America,* published in London in 1789, bears the caption "Americans throwing the Cargoes of the Tea Ships into the River, at Boston." Parliament designed the Tea Act of 1773 as a bailout for the East India Company, but Americans saw it as another attempt to get them to pay a tax levied by a legislature in which they did not enjoy the fundamental right of representation. On December 16, 1773, a select group of Boston's "Sons of Liberty," costumed as Mohawks, boarded the three tea ships and dumped 340 massive chests of tea, valued at £9,000, into Boston Harbor (not "the River" of the caption). The British government responded with the Coercive Acts, which turned the colonial resistance movement into a genuine revolution.

sail. Rather than allow the tea to be unloaded and the duty paid, the local "patriots" clambered aboard the three vessels moored at Griffin's Wharf, winched 340 massive chests of tea up from their holds, then whacked the chests open and spilled the contents into the harbor.

When word of the Tea Party reached London, the ministry led by Lord North decided to make an example of Massachusetts, the colony British officials long deemed the most troublesome to govern. A series of punitive measures soon made their way through Parliament, closing the port of Boston until restitution was made for the tea, altering the royal charter of government for Massachusetts, and allowing soldiers accused of crimes against its citizens to be remanded to Britain for trial. These Coercive or Intolerable Acts were not only offensive in themselves. They also converted the threatening language of the Declaratory Act, asserting that Parliament could legislate for America "in all cases whatsoever," from a statement of principle into a punitive program. In reply, protest meetings across America denounced Parliament and the government of Lord North, and called for an intercolonial Congress (the first since 1765) to coordinate a strategy of resistance.

One of the leading statements of colonial grievances came from the talented quill of Thomas Jefferson, a thirty-one-year-old lawyer and wealthy planter from Virginia. Jefferson's *Summary View of the Rights of British America,* originally composed as instructions to Virginia's delegates to the First Continental Congress, impressed readers with its lucid exposition of the colonists' positions. Jefferson concluded his pamphlet on a brash note. "Open your breast Sire, to liberal and expanded thought," Jefferson wrote. "Let not the name of George the third be a blot in the page of history." How could the king avoid that fate? By dispensing equal justice to his American subjects, and serving as an impartial arbiter between their claims of rights and Parliament's assertion of power.

Jefferson did not attend the eight-week Congress that met in Philadelphia in early September, but its decisions accorded with his advice. Rather than petition Parliament to repeal its legislation, the Continental Congress adopted a stringent declaration of rights to accompany a "loyal address" to the king. Meanwhile it hoped that an uneasy peace could prevail around Boston. There a hapless General Thomas Gage had replaced Thomas Hutchinson as acting governor, with several regiments of British regulars to help enforce the new legislation. With Boston an occupied town, and the surrounding countryside an armed camp of militiamen, Massachusetts had become a tinderbox. In April 1775, after George III had rejected the role Congress had cast him to play, Gage received fresh instructions from London. He was to sortie beyond his Boston bivouac, seize colonial munitions, and arrest patriot leaders like Samuel Adams and John Hancock.

The Revolutionary War began on April 19, 1775, when British troops clashed with local militiamen at Lexington and Concord, west of Boston. In December 1775, Connecticut silversmith Amos Doolittle issued a series of four engraved views of the skirmishes. Here, the third of his engravings, *The Engagement at the North Bridge,* based on a scene by the artist Ralph Earl, depicts the fighting in Concord. Two generations later, in a poem written for the memorial dedication at the North Bridge on July 4, 1837, Ralph Waldo Emerson immortalized the outbreak of war as "the shot heard round the world."

Bloody skirmishes at Lexington and Concord were the immediate result, followed two months later by the fearsome carnage at Bunker Hill.

From this point on, Americans thought they were morally entitled to claim independence, not only from Parliament but also from the king, to whom they still professed loyalty. Obedience and protection, they believed, were reciprocal. A king who made war on his subjects forfeited their allegiance. But it was one thing to believe that independence was morally justifiable, another to conclude that it was politically necessary. A whole year passed before Congress could finally be confident that public opinion favored independence.

The early days of the New Year, 1776, brought news that the king had sharply denounced American protests as the work of traitorous rebels. On January 10, Thomas Paine's sensational pamphlet *Common Sense* appeared—and political debate was never the same. Paine mounted a scathing attack not only on the king but on the entire concept of monarchy, and he joined to it a vigorous defense of the idea of national independence, reminding Americans, for example, that their fears of losing markets for their agricultural exports would remain groundless "so long as eating is the fashion in Europe." As winter gave way to spring, other developments brought the colonists closer to a decision. Individual colonies petitioned Congress for authority to restore lawful government, replacing the apparatus of committees and conventions that had effectively ruled America for the previous year and a half while imperial governors barred most legislatures from meeting, lest they collaborate in resistance. News that the British government had signed treaties for the hire of German mercenaries indicated that it remained committed to a strategy of military repression. To repel British arms, the colonies would need foreign assistance. But what European power would come to their aid until America renounced its formal ties to the mother country?

Responding to these concerns, individual communities and whole provinces began adopting their own resolutions for independence. "Every Post and every Day rolls in upon Us Independence like a Torrent," an exultant John Adams observed on May 20. The most important of these resolutions came from the Virginia Provincial Convention and called for independence, the formation of foreign alliances, and a formal union among the colonies. On Friday, June 7, the Virginia delegate Richard Henry Lee introduced these resolutions to Congress. After two days of intense debate, Congress agreed that the moment for independence was not quite at hand, and postponed action for three weeks. But in the meantime three committees were set to work, preparing a declaration of independence, a plan for foreign treaties, and articles of confederation.

The committee on the declaration numbered five members. The order in which they were listed in the journal of

Congress probably tracks the number of votes each received, so it is notable that Jefferson's name appears first. He had served in Congress since June 1775 and, though not an active or forceful speaker, was much respected for his eloquent writing and for his skills in committee. Second came John Adams, a passionate, irrepressible speaker, and the most outspoken congressional advocate for independence. In this he was fully supported by Benjamin Franklin, the most eminent colonist of the age, and the third delegate chosen to the committee. Its membership was rounded out by Roger Sherman of Connecticut, who had also attended the Stamp Act Congress of 1765, and Robert Livingston, representing the caucus of moderate delegates, primarily from his colony of New York and neighboring Pennsylvania, who still hoped to delay a formal declaration in order to give Britain a final opportunity to offer real terms of accommodation.

Much of what we know about the drafting of the Declaration depends on the recollections that Adams and Jefferson set down decades later. One point of contention is whether the committee asked the two men jointly to make an initial draft, leaving them to hash out a division of labor between them, or whether it asked Jefferson to do so on his own. In a diary entry of 1779, Adams implied that Jefferson was a subcommittee of one. But he took the other line in his autobiography, drafted a quarter-century after that. Now he recalled that there was a subcommittee of two, and that he had insisted Jefferson should do the work, in part because of "the Elegance of his pen," but also because Adams had made himself "obnoxious for my early and constant Zeal in promoting the Measure," which would come under "the more severe Scrutiny and Criticism" if it was known to be his work. Adams was certainly right that Jefferson wielded the more elegant quill. The Massachusetts lawyer could be a vivid and colorful writer, but once inspired, he found it hard to stanch the stream of adjectives that flowed relentlessly from his literary imagination. Not until 1823 did Adams' account of the composition of the Declaration become public knowledge. When it did, Jefferson disputed the claim, recalling that he had indeed been a subcommittee of one. Either way, there is no question that Jefferson was the original author.

Probably acting under guidelines agreed upon in the committee, Jefferson divided the draft into three main sections. First came a preamble of two paragraphs, stating the purpose of the declaration and laying down the fundamental principles that justified the revolutionary actions it was meant to announce. Next came a bill of charges specifically directed against "his present majesty," King George III, but capacious enough to cover other wrongs inflicted by his royal predecessors, including "the cruel war against human nature" waged through the African slave trade. This last charge was, remarkably, the lengthiest of all, dwarfing in passion all the other particulars that explained far more clearly why the

Thomas Jefferson was only thirty-three when he drafted the Declaration of Independence in June 1776. A few weeks earlier he had expressed the wish that he could be given leave to return to Virginia to aid in the great work of writing its new constitution of government. Jefferson was a forty-five-year-old widower, serving as minister to France, when John Trumbull painted this portrait in Paris in 1788.

Americans were rebelling. The third section recapitulated the harsh responses with which the colonists' efforts to vindicate their just rights had been greeted, not only by the British government but also by their "unfeeling brethren" in Britain. Together, these principles, charges, and recriminations justified the conclusion announced in the final paragraph: that the colonies now considered themselves "to be free and independent states," empowered to do everything "which independent states may of right do."

Although the two paragraphs of the preamble contain the passages we remember best, Jefferson saved his most impassioned prose for this concluding third section. His condemnation of George III lacked the sarcastic bite of Tom Paine's pamphlet, but it was just as devastating in assigning responsibility for the decision Americans were about to make. The king was nothing less than a "tyrant," Jefferson wrote, and "future ages will scarce believe that the hardiness of one man" could have committed his government to "so many acts of tyranny without a mask." Taken literally, Jefferson's summation suggests that the king alone carried the burden for the failures of his entire government.

Future ages, with their own experiences of tyrannies the eighteenth century could never imagine, need not take Jefferson's words quite so literally. George III was far more a constitutional monarch than an aspiring despot. For the king to act as Jefferson wished him to do in 1774—become an arbiter between Britain and America—required a statesman-ship that would have set the monarch at odds with the very constitutional principle of parliamentary supremacy he felt morally obliged to defend. Within his own government, it is true, George was very much a hawk, and he fully supported the repressive policy that his ministers had pursued since 1774. But he was hardly the cruel tyrant Jefferson's original language made him out to be.

Jefferson appears to have shown his draft first to Adams, and then to the committee. Franklin, virtually immobilized with gout, probably saw the draft only after his colleagues had reviewed it. Some revisions of wording took place before the Declaration was submitted to Congress on June 28. One notable change substituted the adjective "self-evident"—meaning something more akin to *axiomatic* than merely *obvious*—for the phrase "sacred & undeniable" to describe the fundamental "truths" that Americans commonly believed.

Before the delegates could give their attention to the Declaration, they first had to decide the question of independence itself. Since its inception in 1774, nearly every major decision of Congress had been reached by consensus, and this, its most important act of all, would have to come the same way. When Congress, as scheduled, took up independence on July 1, it found itself just short of the full consensus it sought. Two provinces, the unlikely tandem of Pennsylvania and South Carolina, still opposed total separation, hoping to keep the door to reconciliation ajar. Formal instructions prepared a year earlier bound the New York delegation "to do nothing which should impede" reconciliation, while the two Delaware delegates present "were divided" in sentiment. A decision was postponed until the next day, with the strong hint that South Carolina would then accede. Overnight, Caesar Rodney (the man whose face John Adams memorably described as "not bigger than a large apple") rode up from Delaware to tip the balance in that delegation, while the leading opponents of independence in the Pennsylvania delegation, John Dickinson and Robert Morris, were outmatched by the arrival of new members from their state. It was agreed that the New York delegates would simply abstain. On July 2 Congress adopted Richard Henry Lee's original resolution of June 7 in favor of independence, twelve states to none, with New York abstaining until fresh instructions arrived. An exuberant John Adams wrote to his wife, Abigail, predicting how future generations should treat the second of July. "It ought to be commemorated, as the Day of Deliverance by solemn Acts of Devotion to God Almighty. It ought to be solemnized with Pomp and Parade, with Shews, Games, Sports, Guns, Bells, Bonfires and Illuminations from one End of this Continent to the other from this Time forward forever more." Adams lived long enough to learn that it would be the public rhetoric of Jefferson's Declaration, rather than the political decision that he himself had worked so hard to attain, that Americans would come to commemorate.

With this momentous decision finally taken, Congress turned to the Declaration. Working as a committee of the whole, it did a significant amount of editing over the next two days, producing a more concise text than its drafting committee had generated. Its changes to the first two sections—the preamble and the list of charges against the king—were relatively minor. Then it reached the long paragraph in which Jefferson seemed to foist all of the blame for the African slave trade on George III. Congress deleted the entire passage, and it continued to wield its editorial scalpel as it moved on to the concluding section, with its harsh judgments of the king and the British people. The result was a leaner, tighter, less severe, and arguably more eloquent conclusion. The culprits of the story were still George III, who was "unfit to be the Ruler of a free People" such as the Americans, and his British subjects, for failing to heed "the Voice of Justice and of Consanguinity." But their joint faults were treated less vehemently than Jefferson believed they deserved.

Like any proud author, Jefferson was aggrieved, even bitter, over the "mutilations" his colleagues had carved into his work. But it was intended as a collective declaration, not as his individual pronouncement, and he knew that Congress could be fussy and particular with its public statements. In

1776, Jefferson could not have imagined how closely the document he drafted would be eternally linked to his memory. Nor, if he had, would he have foreseen how much its enduring message would be tied not to the bill of charges against the king, but to those opening two paragraphs, which he thought merely distilled the common sense of the American mind.

There is a deeper irony still to the history of the Declaration and that familiar preamble, and it hinges on the meaning of its best-known phrase, the affirmation "that all men are created equal." Americans have long read those words as a statement about the equality of *individuals*. As such it has long served as an inspiration and rallying cry against the inequalities that one generation has inherited from another yet has come to challenge as unjust, beginning with the nineteenth-century struggles for the abolition of slavery and the recognition of legal rights for women. If we are all created equal, then many of the distinctions and sources of discrimination that law and custom impose on our daily lives can be attacked as unprincipled and arbitrary. Indeed, they deserve to be attacked as a betrayal of the revolutionary promise on which the nation was founded.

Jefferson understood that the phrase could be read this way, and he did envision an American society that would become more egalitarian than the hierarchical world into which he was born and from which he derived such great

personal advantage. Yet when he made equality the founding premise of the Declaration, it was primarily the equality
of *peoples,* not *individuals,* that he meant to assert. The colonists, as a people, had a natural right to enjoy the same rights
of self-government that other peoples did. It was the collective right of revolution and self-government that the Declaration was written to justify—not a visionary or even utopian
notion of equality within American society itself. Yet just as
Jefferson could not prevent Congress from editing his work,
neither could he prevent the citizens and subjects of an independent American nation from reading the Declaration on
their own terms. When they did, it was that statement of
equality that resonated most deeply—until it ultimately became, in Abraham Lincoln's words, "the proposition" to which
the entire nation was "dedicated." This did not mean that
Americans always agreed on the form equality should take,
but it guaranteed that debates about the nature and extent
of equality would always figure prominently in their politics.

The members of the Continental Congress who approved
the Declaration were confident they were speaking for their
constituents in the thirteen states. Their act culminated a
decade of protests against imperial policy and two years
of political crisis and military conflict. The framers of the
Constitution were far less certain that the American people
would accept the reforms they proposed. Five more years

of hard, sometimes desperate military conflict followed the Declaration of Independence, until victory at Yorktown in October 1781 brought an end to active military operations in North America. In April 1783 Congress ratified the peace treaty that John Jay, Benjamin Franklin, and John Adams negotiated at Paris. Whether the next four years of peace were a truly "critical period" is a question historians still debate, and probably always will. But by 1787 most Americans seemed to agree that the Articles of Confederation, the nation's first federal constitution, was badly defective. Every effort to amend it had failed, and there was no public consensus as to what amendments should be adopted.

There were thus significant differences between the political circumstances of 1776 and 1787. In its origins, the Constitution was the product not of a popular movement clamoring for change, but of a small group of influential leaders whose ideas ran far ahead of what the public seemed to want. Yet their ideas also reflected a decade of hard-won experience under the new constitutions of government that Americans began adopting in 1776. The immediate occasion for the Convention of 1787 was the weakness of national government under the Articles of Confederation. But the defects of the state constitutions and the mistaken policies of individual states were very much on the minds of its leading framers, especially the young Virginian, James Madison, who did the most to set the convention's agenda.

To understand why this was the case, it is important to recognize that the Articles of Confederation and the Constitution embodied two distinct models of federalism, that peculiarly complicated creature which tries to divide the sovereign powers of government between a central authority and member provinces that retain some substantial degree of autonomy. As proposed in 1777 and finally ratified in 1781, the Articles of Confederation left the states with full legal authority over their "internal police," meaning every aspect of governance that affected the lives, property, and welfare of their citizens. The sole constitutional organ of national government was the unicameral Continental Congress (or more properly, the "United States in Congress Assembled"), where each state cast one vote, regardless of differences in population. Its principal duties were the conduct of war and diplomacy. In this sense, Congress did embody the national sovereignty of the United States, but it was a national sovereign that could not make law for its own citizens. Members of Congress were elected by the state legislatures, not the people, and as such they could not be trusted with the ordinary authority of representatives to enact statutes and levy taxes. Instead, Congress relied on the states to carry out many of its decisions. Congress would issue resolutions, recommendations, and, most important, requisitions for revenue, men, and supplies—directives which the states in good faith were expected to execute or fulfill. In general, the states did their best to comply. But the demands and burdens of the war were overwhelming, and the state legislatures were fearful of alienating the political loyalty of their citizens by taxing them too strenuously.

Modest efforts to amend the Confederation began as soon as it took effect. In 1781 and again in 1783, Congress sought authority to collect duties on foreign imports, so that it would acquire an independent source of revenue that it could use to secure foreign loans. In 1784 it also sought limited authority to regulate foreign commerce, the better to retaliate against the discriminatory policies Britain was pursuing against American merchants. None of these amendments gained the unanimous approval of the state legislatures that the Confederation required. In September 1786, at the invitation of Virginia, a group of twelve commissioners from five states gathered at Mann's Tavern in Annapolis to discuss an amendment vesting Congress with new authority over trade. Believing their numbers too few to act but unwilling to disband without doing something, the Annapolis commissioners played a risky gambit. A new convention of the states should meet in Philadelphia in May 1787, they proposed, and its agenda should extend to the defects of the Confederation as a whole. Having agreed on this point, the commissioners returned to their states to lobby for their daring proposal. The first to act was the "ancient dominion" of Virginia, the nation's most populous state.

Of the dozen commissioners, Madison was the one who took this invitation most seriously, as both a political duty and intellectual challenge. Like his fellow commissioner Alexander Hamilton, he was part of the generation that came of age with the Revolution. In the spring of 1776, just turned twenty-five, Madison attended the provincial convention that wrote Virginia's first constitution. Service in the new legislature and council of state was followed by three and a half years of uninterrupted attendance at Congress (1780–1783), then another three years as the dominant figure in the Virginia assembly (1784–1786).

From this experience at both the national and state levels of government, Madison could draw lessons aplenty about what he called the "vices of the political system of the U. States." *How* he drew those lessons reveals much about his distinct political talents. Relying on a "literary cargo" of books sent to him by Jefferson (now serving as envoy to France), Madison began a course of reading in the history of ancient and modern confederacies. But to this academic inquiry he added a powerful set of reflections rooted in the frustrations he had encountered as a member first of Congress and then of the Virginia assembly. Those experiences persuaded him that any system of federalism based on the idea that the states would freely comply with the recommendations of Congress was doomed to failure. What was needed instead, he concluded, was a national government

James Madison, one of the Revolution's "young men," is often called the "Father of the Constitution" for both his far-reaching vision of the new federal government and his unflagging efforts at the Federal Convention of 1787. This miniature was painted by Charles Willson Peale in 1783, when Madison was courting Kitty Floyd, daughter of a New York congressman. She dropped him for a medical student, and eleven years passed before Madison married the widow Dolley Payne Todd in September 1794.

that would act directly on the people through the ordinary mechanisms of law. To be true to sound constitutional principles, such a government would have to be radically restructured. In place of a unicameral Congress, it would have to take the form that Americans expected to see in all well-designed governments: a bicameral legislature and an independent executive and judiciary.

At home in Virginia, Madison quickly persuaded the assembly to issue a fresh invitation to the other state legislatures to appoint delegations for Philadelphia. Virginia's own delegation would be top-heavy with talent. In addition to Madison and his even younger friend, Governor Edmund Randolph, it included George Mason, the chief author of the state's constitution of 1776 and its accompanying declaration of rights; George Wythe, long-time professor of law at the College of William and Mary (and Jefferson's mentor); and George Washington. The last appointment was the most important and most delicate. Upon resigning his commission as commander-in-chief in December 1783, Washington had also declared his firm intention to return forever to private life. To violate that pledge, even for so patriotic a purpose, might blemish the "character" Washington had worked so hard to earn and remained so keen to protect. Yet the general also ranked first among those who supported the project of effective national governance. After all, no one had a keener experience of the costs of relying on the states to answer national needs. His entire military command had been one continuous struggle to persuade Congress and the states to keep his army well manned, well armed, well clothed, and well fed.

Seven states had endorsed the Philadelphia meeting by

February 1787. Congress removed a critical obstacle by adding its own approval on February 21. Eventually, all but Rhode Island agreed to attend, and the absence of that minuscule state proved a blessing in disguise. A state that could not be troubled even to send a delegation seemed unlikely to approve anything the convention proposed. But this made it easier for the delegates to abandon the amendment rules of the Confederation and consider whether the assent of fewer than thirteen states would be enough to ensure the adoption of whatever changes they proposed.

One other event in New England shaped the delegates' thinking about the challenge they faced. This was Shays's Rebellion, a militant protest by western Massachusetts farmers against the high taxes their government had levied in a good-faith effort to retire the state's wartime debt. Farmers who failed to pay their taxes risked having their property sold at auction. A show of force by the militia quelled the protest, but its supporters regrouped at the spring elections, replacing the governor who had suppressed the rebellion with the more popular John Hancock. Massachusetts was regarded as one of the best-governed states in the Union; if it could experience such turmoil, the American experiment in republican government seemed destined to end, like other republics, in turbulence and anarchy. Or so at least some members of the propertied classes—like Madison—naturally feared.

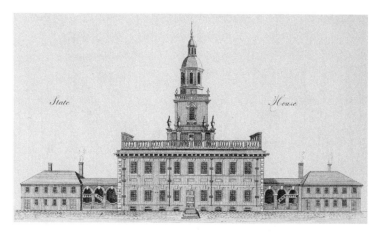

This engraving shows the State House (Independence Hall) in Philadelphia as it looked to the founders. The engraving originally appeared as an inset on John Reed's *Map of Philadelphia and Vicinity* (1774). Architects consider it the most accurate eighteenth-century depiction of the building. While the Federal Convention met in the main room downstairs, the Pennsylvania assembly generously moved its sessions to the floor above.

May 14, 1787, was the appointed day of meeting, but it came and went with only the two host delegations—Virginia (as the inviting state) and Pennsylvania—present. Heavy spring rains were one source of the delay, but so were the dilatory habits of eighteenth-century public bodies. Not until May 25 did a quorum of seven states finally muster. The Virginians used the interval to advantage, meeting "two or three hours a day, in order to form a proper correspondence of sen-

Like farmers in other states, farmers in western Massachusetts were struggling with high debt and taxes after the Revolution. Dissidents rallied behind the figure of Daniel Shays, a former captain in the Continental Army. In the uprising known as Shays's Rebellion, they forced the closing of courts and released debtors from prison. Shays and his followers were defeated in battle in February 1787, but to many the armed uprising demonstrated the need for a stronger national government. In this illustration from *Bickerstaff's Genuine Boston Almanack for 1787*, Shays is portrayed on the left, and another prominent Shaysite, Job Shattuck, is on the right.

timents" among themselves. More important, they drafted a set of eleven articles that the delegation's titular head, Governor Edmund Randolph, presented to the convention on May 29. The basis for this Virginia Plan could be found in letters and one critical memorandum that Madison had drafted in the early spring. Madison's program called for the establishment of a supreme national government comprising three independent departments, including a bicameral legislature in which representation in *both* houses would be allocated among the states in proportion to population and perhaps some unspecified measure of wealth. The legislature would be authorized to act "in all cases to which the separate States are incompetent, or in which the harmony of the United States may be interrupted by the exercise of individual Legislation." Madison probably expected that this open-ended grant of legislative *authority* would eventually give way to a list of specific legislative *powers*. But the fact that the Virginia Plan could propose this at all was a measure of the radical change it contemplated.

Taken together, these proposals would free the national government from its crippling dependence on the states. But privately Madison had concluded that the convention should go further and use the occasion of *national* reform to strike at another problem: what he called the "multiplicity," "mutability," and "injustice" of lawmaking within the individual *states*. He had grown highly alarmed about the adoption of

Reproduced here is the opening passage from Madison's "Vices of the Political System of the United States" (April 1787). In this memorandum, drafted only weeks prior to the Federal Convention, we see Madison's mind at work. His analysis of the "vices" or deficiencies of the Articles of Confederation provided him with a working agenda for the Federal Convention in Philadelphia. This is a great document in the history of political ideas, for it reveals a creative thinker trying to solve real problems of constitutional design.

paper money and debtor relief laws which, he feared, might violate fundamental rights of property; he even worried that legislatures that were too responsive to popular influence might soon adopt redistributionist policies that would transfer wealth from one class to another. His most radical proposal of all was thus to give the national legislature a negative (or veto) over state laws. Had it been adopted, that proposal would have stripped the states of any claim to being sovereign authorities in the conventional meaning of the term.

Madison believed he could justify these changes on the basis of experience and theory alike. But his strategy for the convention rested on one other, deeply political calculation. The most populous states would accept these radical reforms only if the old rule of "one state, one vote" was abandoned, not only in the lower house but in the upper house as well. The less populous states (Delaware, Maryland, New Hampshire, Connecticut) would naturally resist this change, but Madison believed that forceful argument and sheer necessity would ultimately overcome their opposition. If the delegations speaking for the populous states maintained a united front, he calculated, "the lesser States must in every event yield to the predominant will."

That calculation set the tone for the first six weeks of the deliberations that began after Governor Randolph presented the Virginia Plan on May 29. Perhaps the convention might have proceeded differently had the other delegations arrived promptly, and not allowed the Virginians to take advantage of their absence. A few delegates suggested that they should first decide how powerful a government they wanted to create before tackling the thorny question of representation. But Madison and his allies insisted that everything hinged on that one issue.

To facilitate candid discussions, the convention initially sat as a committee of the whole. This spared Washington from having to occupy the presiding chair to which he was immediately and unanimously elected. Meeting as a committee enabled the delegates to try out ideas and adopt positions that they could later modify or abandon. The convention spent its first fortnight working its way through the Virginia Plan. On some points it made quick progress. Over a handful of dissents, it agreed to vest the executive power in a single person, the better to assign and assure responsibility for the management of government. Remarkably, too, it also agreed to give the executive a veto over legislation, a power generally denied to the governors under the new state constitutions written in 1776.

In discussing this point, the delegates also revealed their understanding of the emerging idea of judicial review, the key doctrine which enables the judiciary to decide whether legislative acts and some executive actions meet constitutional standards. The Virginia Plan included a proposal to submit pending legislation to a joint executive-judicial council of revision, modeled on a similar feature in the constitution of New York. In criticizing this proposal, some delegates argued that it was improper to involve judges in lawmaking at all; others noted that the right time for judges to test the constitutionality of legislation would come when they had to try actual legal controversies. Alluding to a handful of recent cases in state courts, they clearly understood that judicial review—the power to declare laws void for constitutional reasons—was a legitimate function of a properly constructed judiciary.

The representation question, however, overshadowed everything else. From the outset, delegates from the less populous states made it plain that they would not be cowed into submission. They gained an early point in their favor on June 7, when the convention readily agreed that the upper house should be appointed by the state legislatures. Although that did not rule out apportioning seats on the basis of population, it did imply that the upper house would somehow represent states per se—and each state was equally a state, regardless of population. A week later the small states countered the ambitious scope of the Virginia Plan with the New Jersey Plan, which proposed adding new powers to the existing Congress while leaving the equal state vote intact. The delegates dispatched the New Jersey Plan after a debate lasting less than three days—one of which was spent listening to Alexander Hamilton's famous if idiosyncratic speech praising the British constitution and suggesting that their real object should be to emulate it as closely as possible. An executive and an upper house serving for life, Hamilton thought, would be a useful antidote to the republican prejudice in favor of annual rotation in office.

The New Jersey Plan was less a serious alternative to the

Virginia Plan than a way of proving that the small states remained deeply committed to the equal state vote. Their delegates insisted that the welfare and even the very existence of the small states would be at risk if they accepted a government based on a rule of proportional representation. Madison thought the best way to refute this claim was to prove that the small states neither deserved nor needed that security. They did not *deserve* it because an equal state vote would unjustly give small states a disproportionate influence. They did not *need* it because, in fact, the size of a state had no bearing on the real interests of its citizens. Look at the three largest states (Virginia, Pennsylvania, and Massachusetts), Madison and his allies pointedly asked. What interests did they share that would enable them to form a ruling coalition? The short answer was none, and the small states could never quite explain what they feared, other than a reduction of influence and the loss of a privilege they enjoyed under the Confederation. But that did not stop them from keeping a united front.

Another round of debates on this issue ended on July 2, when the convention deadlocked on a motion to give the states an equal vote in the upper house. Over Madison's objections, the delegates then appointed a committee to prepare a compromise. After joining the other delegates in marking the eleventh anniversary of independence, the committee brought in its report on July 5. The committee proposed a three-part compromise. First, seats in the lower house would be apportioned among the states on the basis of population, with each slave "rated" at three-fifths of a free person. Second, "all bills for raising and appropriating money" would originate in the lower house, and not be subject to alteration in the upper house. Third, in the upper house "each State shall have an equal Vote." Madison and his allies immediately dismissed this proposal as no compromise at all. The concession relating to appropriations meant nothing, they scoffed, so long as the assent of the upper house was still needed for such measures to pass.

The committee's first resolution prompted several days of bickering, which was aggravated by the efforts of two additional committees to propose an initial allocation of seats in the lower house. Some delegates favored basing representation on some combination of persons and property. A few northern delegates argued that slaves should never be counted for purposes of representation. Gouverneur Morris of Pennsylvania had an even more radical idea: all the seaboard states, north and south, should band together to assure that they would always retain the advantage in representation, regardless of the prospective movement of population westward into the interior. The best way to do that was to leave it to the national legislature to determine when and how to reapportion. But believing (wrongly, as it turned out) that future population movements would bring their region closer to parity with the North, and that slavery should be factored into the representation equation, southern delegates argued that the three-fifths rule should be retained, that regular reapportionment should be constitutionally required, and that, to make it effective, a national census should be taken at fixed intervals. Some northern delegates remained troubled by the idea of counting slaves for purposes of representation. American law treated slaves primarily as property, not persons; and representation, they further argued, was in its origins a substitute for collective meetings of the people that slaves would never attend or where they would never speak or vote.

The convention spent several days wrangling over this issue before finally adopting the three-fifths rule—and even then it took two subterfuges to carry the point. One was that the words "slave" and "slavery" would not be used. The other was that the rule of representation would also cover the formula for apportioning direct taxes (such as poll or land taxes, as opposed to customs duties or excises) among the states. But most delegates doubted that the national government would resort to direct taxes; this was simply a way to suggest that the southern states would pay for as well as benefit from their ownership of slaves.

With that question resolved, the delegates finally returned to the question of the equal state vote in the Senate. After six weeks of impasse, there were no new arguments to make, and few minds were open to change. But it took only two weak links in the Massachusetts delegation to prove that the stubbornness of the small states had outlasted the better arguments of the large. In the decisive vote of July 16, Elbridge Gerry and Caleb Strong opted for compromise, perhaps fearing that the small states would fulfill their threat to walk out should the convention deprive them of an equal vote in at least one house. Their defection split the Massachusetts delegation and allowed the equal state vote to pass by the narrow margin of five states to four, with one divided.

The large-state advocates were so disconcerted by this setback that they were unprepared to proceed. After an adjournment overnight they caucused the next morning, only to discover that they could not agree on a strategy to undo their defeat. The small states had called Madison's bluff, or at least proved impervious to his superior arguments, and there was no choice but to forge ahead.

The famous decision of July 16, which we mistakenly label a compromise and wrongly attribute to Connecticut, had four major consequences. First, it led immediately to the rejection of the Virginia Plan's proposed congressional negative on state laws. Acceptance of the idea that the states as such were important enough to be equally represented implied that their laws should not be subjected to strict national scrutiny. Second, it cleared the path for the delegates to turn their attention to other neglected issues, particularly the executive. Third, it encouraged the convention to replace the Virginia Plan's broad grant of legislative power with an enumerated set of particular powers. Fourth, and arguably most important, it guaranteed that the American constitutional system would forever fall short of the "one person, one vote" rule that is a defining norm of modern democracy. For some purposes, some citizens remain more equal than others, not because they are wiser or more patriotic, or because their interests deserve special recognition, but simply because the accident of their residence in less populous states gives them a bigger political bang for their electoral buck.

The executive was the next major item on the delegates' agenda, and they spent much of the next week and a half in a puzzled discussion of how to elect or appoint the single person who would wield the "executive power." There were two obvious possibilities—election by the legislature or by the people—and one contrived alternative that grew attractive whenever the defects of the other methods became apparent, which they quickly did. Election by the legislature had the advantage of leaving the choice up to the nation's best-informed leaders. But because the framers were intent on making the president politically independent of the legislature, the victorious candidate could serve only a single term, lest he become a toady to a dominant faction—which would seem to deny the republic the potential benefit of experience gained in office. Popular election posed two major problems.

First, it would clearly favor candidates from northern states, because with a single national constituency, the enslavement of much of the southern population would always make the free citizens of the North a majority of the electorate. More important, the framers worried that voters would naturally prefer candidates from their own states and ignore contenders from others, making it difficult for anyone to gain a majority without some costly cycle of repeated elections.

In response to these doubts, the framers hit upon the idea of appointing a select corps of electors, well-informed citizens who might make a knowledgeable choice without gaining any lasting political influence of their own. For a moment this notion became almost a panacea—until the framers started doubting that these electors "would be men of the first or even the second rank." The delegates finished this round of debate where they began it, with an executive appointed by the legislature for a single term of seven years.

On July 26, after two months of deliberations, the convention recessed after appointing a committee of detail to convert the resolutions adopted thus far into a working draft of a constitution. The Pennsylvania delegate Robert Morris took his distinguished houseguest, George Washington, to fish at Valley Forge, but soon the general's memories pulled him away from his tackle to wander among the huts his bedraggled men had hastily erected in that bitter winter of 1778. When the delegates reassembled on August 6, the committee presented a draft of twenty-three articles, many containing provisions the convention had never discussed. For the first time the legislature was called "Congress," keeping the name of the discredited institution it would replace. Its two chambers received their permanent names of Senate and House of Representatives, while the chief executive was given the "Stile" of "the President of the United States" and the "title" of "his Excellency." The committee's report also enumerated powers that belonged to each institution. Instead of a grant of general legislative authority, Congress would have a set of specific powers, beginning with the critical power to levy and collect taxes and to regulate foreign and interstate commerce. The Senate was given the power to make treaties and appoint ambassadors and Supreme Court justices, while the president would appoint other officers. His chief responsibility, however, was to "take care that the laws of the United States be duly and faithfully executed." This was the core *republican* definition of executive power, a definition that emphasized responsibility over initiative.

Over the next five weeks, the convention worked through these resolutions. Either the pace of debate quickened, or Madison was worn down by his self-appointed task of keeping a running account of the debates. His notes for these weeks record few lengthy speeches and many snappier exchanges. The chief development of this final round of deliberation was a gradual but marked growth of presidential power. Much of it was driven not by a bold vision of the virtues of an energetic executive, but rather by second thoughts about the Senate—a body which looked disturbingly like the old Congress. In a key vote in late August, the convention deadlocked on the legislative election of the president, and that vexing question was soon assigned to the curiously named Committee on Postponed Parts, chaired by the normally quiet Jonathan Dayton of New Jersey.

Its report of September 4 proposed two sets of changes that gave shape to the presidency. The first transferred the power to make treaties and all major appointments to the president, acting with the advice and consent of the Senate. The second created the electoral scheme that came to be known as the Electoral College—a college that could never meet as one deliberative body, but could gather only as separate faculties in the individual states, vote on the same day, and then disband. The electoral scheme combined the two major decisions on representation, which the framers, their tempers having cooled, were now more disposed to treat as compromises than they had been in July. Each state would get a number of electors equal to its total membership in Congress. The most populous states would have the advantage in promoting the candidates they favored, or at least in making front-runners. In the event that no candidate received a majority of electoral votes—a situation which many delegates thought would be the rule rather than the exception—the choice would devolve on the Senate, where the states would vote equally. Incumbents would also be free to seek reelection.

But here lay a problem: the Senate and president were now going to share the treaty-making and appointment powers. How could the president exercise independent judgment when decisions in these areas needed the approval of the body that had already elected and would possibly reelect him? It took three days of debate for Roger Sherman to hit upon an ingenious scheme: let the House select a president from the five leading candidates to emerge from the first round of electoral voting, but require its members to vote as delegations rather than individuals, so that each state would have one vote. This allowed the Electoral College to replicate the earlier compromises over representation while allowing the president to remain politically independent of the Senate.

Many modern commentators fault the framers for making the president too independent of Congress. In mature parliamentary democracies, the executive (or, literally, the government) stays in power only so long as it commands majority support in the legislature, while strong political parties generally enable the executive to keep the legislature in line, until such time as the governing ministers lose legislators' confidence or elections bring a new party or coalition to power. In the United States, by contrast, the staggered terms for representatives, senators, and the president make effective governance more difficult and divided government more likely. The framers' commitment to separating the powers — or, more specifically, separating the political branches — may be their most durable and vexing legacy, at least when we pay close attention to the structure of the government they created.

Perhaps. But before we fault them too much, we should recall the difficulties they faced. The two dominant models of executive power in the eighteenth century were monarchical or ministerial, and Americans profoundly disliked both. Nor was there any useful precedent for choosing a national executive by popular election. Only Massachusetts and New York elected governors by popular vote. Even in Britain, the outcomes of elections did not yet determine who controlled the government; kings still had a substantial say in the choice of ministers; and the existence of a primitive form of cabinet government, Americans believed, often shielded ministers from parliamentary or public scrutiny. The framers could hardly reject a form of parliamentary democracy that did not yet exist. Given these conditions, it is not surprising that they found it difficult to grasp the political dimensions of executive power, particularly in designing the constitution of a republic — a form of government that valued collective deliberation over concentrated decision making.

With the presidency finally resolved, the convention spent a few more days tying up loose ends, then turned the document over to a committee of style whose dominant member was Gouverneur Morris of Pennsylvania. As a young man back in the mid-1770s, Morris had broken with his Loyalist family to support the American cause, then moved quickly into the patriot elite in his native New York. Later he served as assistant to Robert Morris (no relation), the superintendent of finance who first tried to whip continental finances into manageable shape in the early 1780s. As constitutional editor, Gouverneur Morris performed some radical surgery of his own, compressing the twenty-three resolutions of the committee of detail into seven carefully defined articles, each with its own proper subject, and even altering language and punctuation. The result was a more dignified document that encourages some commentators to look for clues to its meaning in its structure, literary polish, and textual echoes.

The convention held its last session on September 17. First, its presiding officer, an otherwise silent Washington, made an unprecedented intervention to support a last-minute reduction in the ratio of population to representation in the House. No one dared to gainsay him, and the

GOVERNEER MORRIS ESQ.ʀ

Member of Congress.

Pub.ᵈ 15ᵗʰ May 1783 by R. Wilkinson N.º 58 Cornhill London

Pennsylvania delegate Gouverneur Morris (1752–1816) was the leading member of the committee of style that prepared the final draft of the Constitution. Morris took the twenty-three articles the Convention had approved and gave the Constitution its final structure of seven articles and subordinate sections and clauses. This engraving, dated May 15, 1783, is by R. Wilkinson.

change was adopted. Then the convention's other great luminary, Benjamin Franklin, made a final plea for unanimity to the three delegates who had already declared their opposition to the Constitution. Unwilling to accept the common sense of America's great sage, Randolph, Gerry, and Mason still held out, and watched silently as the other delegates proceeded to sign. Then the delegates adjourned as Franklin offered one last quip, noting that he now believed it was a rising sun, not a setting one, that adorned the chair from which Washington had presided over nearly four months of deliberation, the most sustained experiment in constitution making the world had yet known.

The ratification campaign began almost immediately. Among its many decisions, the convention agreed that its work should not be subject to the amendment rules of the Confederation. In deference to Congress, the Constitution would be sent there first—but only so Congress could then quickly transmit it, unaltered, to the states. Nor would the state legislatures be allowed to judge the Constitution on its merits. Their sole task was to provide for the election of the separate ratification conventions. The Constitution would take effect with the approval of nine conventions, rather than thirteen legislatures. These conventions would have to approve or reject it in its entirety, not accept some articles while trying to revise others. Some states might opt out of the new federal union, but those that joined would do so with a single unequivocal act. The approval procedures of Article VII provided a brilliantly simple solution to a potentially difficult problem.

The framers themselves took the lead in mobilizing the coalitions that spent much of the next year debating and contesting the Constitution. A number of delegates, led by Madison, immediately returned to New York City, the nation's capital since 1785, to ensure that Congress would promptly submit the Constitution to the states. Others, like James Wilson of Pennsylvania, Alexander Hamilton of New York, and Rufus King of Massachusetts, took the lead in making sure that their state legislatures answered the call to arrange elections for the ratification conventions. The Federalist supporters of the Constitution had the great advantage of rallying around one simple goal, and, in doing so, being able to contrast the promise of effective government under the Constitution with the manifest "imbecility" of Congress under the Confederation.

Much of the Federalist case for ratification rested on appeals to the promise of peace and prosperity under the Constitution and the prestige of Washington and Franklin, two luminaries who would never betray the national interest. But in New York, Alexander Hamilton launched an ambitious effort to prepare a comprehensive brief for ratification, one that would begin with general arguments for strengthening the federal union, but then defend the proposed Constitu-

tion, article by article and even clause by clause. First he re-
cruited his fellow New Yorker John Jay, the secretary of foreign affairs, and then he signed up Madison. Ill health kept
Jay from contributing more than a handful of essays, but
Madison added twenty-nine to the lion's share composed
by Hamilton (fifty-one). Writing collectively under the pen
name "Publius" and the title *The Federalist,* the coauthors
provided the first systematic commentary on the Constitution and left posterity a work that is generally regarded as
the new republic's most important and distinctively American contribution to the canon of political theory. That it was
composed as the eighteenth-century equivalent of a running
series of op-ed pieces speaks volumes for the brilliance of its
authors.

On the other side, the Anti-Federalist opponents of the
Constitution drew upon a suspicion of centralized power
that was already deeply rooted in American political culture.
Adoption of the Constitution, they argued, would lead to a
"consolidation" of all real authority in a distant national government whose members would lack "sympathy" with the
interests and concerns of ordinary citizens. Anti-Federalists
saw dangers lurking everywhere in the text. The power to
tax would give the national government a monopoly over every easy source of revenue, leaving the states to depend on
the more obnoxious forms of taxation that Americans hated
most. Under the "Necessary and Proper" Clause, Congress

In the PRESS,
and ſpeedily will be publiſhed,
THE
FEDERALIST,
A Collection of Eſſays written in fa
vor of the New Conſtitution.
By a Citizen of New-York.
Corrected by the Author, with Additions
and Alterations.

*This work will be printed on a fine Paper
and good Type, in one handſome Volume duo-
decimo, and delivered to ſubſcribers at the
moderate price of one dollar. A few copies
will be printed on ſuperfine royal writing paper, price ten ſhillings.
No money required till delivery.*

*To render this work more complete, will be
added, without any additional expence,*

PHILO-PUBLIUS,
AND THE
Articles of the Convention,
*As agreed upon at Philadelphia, Septem-
ber 17th, 1787.*

Writing under the pen name "Publius" and the simple title of *The Federalist,*
coauthors Alexander Hamilton, John Jay, and James Madison published eighty-
five essays in support of the Constitution. The essays first appeared two or
three times weekly in New York newspapers from October 1787 to May 1788
and then were reprinted in a two-volume edition by the New York pub-
lishers J. and A. McLean. This is an advertisement for that edition. Modern
readers will note that our squat letter *s* appears only at the end of words; all
other uses take the form of that strange *f*-like character we find so charming—
or distracting.

could legislate on any subject it wished, bypassing the specific enumeration of its legislative powers. The Supremacy Clause would allow the national government to run roughshod over state laws. The president might turn into a monarch, or the Senate might use its terrifying combination of legislative, executive, and judicial powers to dominate the other branches. A Supreme Court anxious to enlarge its docket would find ways to encourage Congress to legislate. The whole Constitution seemed to be a parade of horribles.

Anti-Federalists have been described as "men of little faith," early examples of what Richard Hofstadter once memorably characterized as the "paranoid style in American politics." Yet in expressing their concerns, they also drew upon some of the best political science of the age, notably the writings of "the celebrated Montesquieu" (as Madison described him in *Federalist* 47), the eminent French *philosophe* whose great work, *The Spirit of the Laws,* deeply influenced the American constitution-writers of 1776. It was Montesquieu who first formulated the modern theory of the separation of powers into distinct legislative, executive, and judicial branches—a theory that Anti-Federalists believed the Constitution badly violated. He was commonly associated with another established principle that the Constitution seemed to transgress. This was the idea that a stable republic could exist only in small, relatively homogeneous societies

Supporters of the Constitution had to reckon with the great intellectual legacy of the French philosopher and satirist Charles-Louis de Secondat, baron de La Brède et de Montesquieu (1689–1755). His great work of political science, *De L'Esprit des lois* (published anonymously in 1748 and translated in a widely read English edition as *The Spirit of the Laws* in 1750), laid down two principles that the Constitution was accused of violating. One was that republican governments worked best in small homogeneous societies, like the ancient Greek city-states. The other was that power had to be carefully divided into separate departments. Madison and Hamilton devoted key passages of *The Federalist* to explaining why Montesquieu was either wrong or was being misread. This portrait by an anonymous French artist was painted in 1728.

whose virtuous citizens would know how to subordinate their private interests to the greater public good.

The opponents of the Constitution, then, had good reason to argue that the Philadelphia convention had simply gone too far, and their objections resonated with popular opinion. Yet their campaign against ratification was badly coordinated, and they struggled to get their views adequately published in many newspapers. Then, too, their strategic goal proved hard to define. Was it to block adoption of the Constitution outright or accept it with alterations? And if the latter, which ones? Americans seemed so disillusioned with the "imbecility" of the Confederation that they could hardly be expected to rally to its preservation. Yet wouldn't that be the most likely consequence of rejecting the Constitution?

The political momentum thus belonged to the Federalists, and they worked hard to keep it. They notched early, easy victories in five states: Delaware, Georgia, Pennsylvania, New Jersey, and Connecticut. Massachusetts, meeting early in 1788, provided the first serious test. There Anti-Federalists appeared to have a majority, and it took some maneuvering to work out a deal whereby the convention would ratify the Constitution while *recommending* a set of amendments for future consideration. This solution set a precedent for other states where Federalists needed to placate their opponents without abandoning their great goal. The key to their strategy was to insist that all acts of ratification had to be conclusive and unequivocal. State conventions could recommend as many amendments as they wished, but they could not adopt the Constitution on a contingent basis, by withholding final assent until the desired changes were proposed, either by the new Congress or in a second convention.

This strategy proved crucial to Federalist success in New Hampshire, Virginia, and New York, the ninth, tenth, and eleventh states to ratify the Constitution in the early summer of 1788. Rhode Island had already rejected it, uniquely by popular referendum. The North Carolina convention, the last to meet, rejected as well, but it also proposed amendments whose adoption might entice it to rejoin the Union. The amendments the states proposed covered a whole array of subjects. Many were concerned with the substantive powers and institutional structure of the government. But one recurring criticism of the Constitution was its lack of a list of fundamental rights, akin to the declarations that accompanied many of the state constitutions. The issue had come up briefly at Philadelphia, at the instigation of the two nonsigners, George Mason and Elbridge Gerry, but the framers dismissed it out of hand with only cursory debate.

This proved a serious miscalculation, but not a fatal one. When it seemed necessary to do so, Federalists agreed that additional articles protecting fundamental rights could be considered as possible amendments. But with the Constitution safely ratified and the country beginning to prepare for elections to put it into effect, many Federalists thought they were not obliged to pursue amendments at all. The outcome of the winter elections strengthened that opinion. Federalists captured decisive majorities in both houses of Congress, George Washington would be the first president, and it seemed entirely possible that a successful launch of the new government would dissipate Anti-Federalist fears. But one leading Federalist dissented from this rosy view. In Virginia, James Madison had reluctantly acceded to the Anti-Federalist demand to propose amendments. Then, in a tough race against his friend James Monroe for election to the House of Representatives, he issued public letters indicating he would personally take the lead in shepherding amendments through Congress. Madison enjoyed important political support from the dissenting Baptists in his district, and Baptists were deeply committed to the free exercise of religious liberty. By publicly indicating his willingness to support the addition of an article protecting that and other fundamental rights, Madison helped secure his election to the House of Representatives.

Once elected, Madison took that pledge seriously. But at the same time, he was firmly determined not to alter any of the substantive provisions the framers had worked so hard to compile. The institutions of government would remain just as the framers designed them. Nor would there be any change in the powers the national government wielded. After reviewing all the amendments the state conventions had proposed, Madison limited his proposed revisions almost exclusively to providing a statement of rights. Privately he continued to think that such declarations were so many "parchment barriers" that did little to protect the rights they proclaimed. In his view, the greatest dangers to rights would arise not from arbitrary acts of power-hungry rulers but from the impassioned feelings of the people themselves—or rather, from the selfish interests and partial opinions of popular majorities and the elected representatives who would cater to them. And Madison remained deeply skeptical that bills of rights would effectively restrain either the people or their leaders. But he also thought there were many well-meaning if misguided Anti-Federalists who did believe that a Constitution lacking a bill of rights was defective, and it was important to allay their doubts to ensure that the Constitution would truly take effect.

Once the new Congress slowly assembled in New York City in the early spring of 1789, Madison gave notice of his intention to introduce amendments. Not until June 8, however, did he actually present them to the House, and even then he half apologized for distracting it from other urgent subjects. True to his fears, the House was slow to take up his proposals. A good six weeks passed before the House assigned Madison's amendments to a select committee.

Once appointed, the select committee (which included Madison) worked quickly, and within a week it brought a revised version of Madison's proposals back to the House. Over the objections of Roger Sherman of Connecticut, the committee agreed with Madison on one key textual matter: that the new clauses should be inserted at those points in the existing Constitution where they seemed most salient. Sherman objected that Congress had no right to alter the original text produced by the Convention of 1787, but could only add to it. Madison believed, however, that interweaving the new clauses with the old would better indicate exactly how the rights in question were to be protected. For the moment, his view prevailed.

Another fortnight passed before the House took up the report. By now, Madison had taken to calling his proposals "the nauseous project of amendments," something he still had to force down the throats of reluctant colleagues. After a week of debate, the House finally swallowed the medicine, and sent a package of seventeen amendments to the Senate. It made two significant changes to Madison's scheme, however. First, it eliminated a statement of natural rights that Madison had intended to operate, in effect, as a second preamble to the entire Constitution. Second, after extensive discussion, the House finally endorsed Sherman's view that the amendments should appear as supplemental articles, not interwoven clauses. Over the long run, this made it easier for later interpreters to regard the amendments as a Bill of Rights with an intellectual coherence of its own—in a sense, a semi-autonomous section of the Constitution with its own purpose and logic. Over the short run, Madison worried that this detached format would leave ambiguous whose responsibility it was to see that the rights mentioned were protected, or precisely where the threat to particular rights originated. But in his mind, the real purpose of the amendments remained political: to assuage Anti-Federalist qualms and put a final seal of approval on the whole process of ratification.

By now it was late August, and with everyone eager to adjourn, the Senate acted much more quickly than the House. It received the House proposals on August 24 and returned them three weeks later. It, too, made one significant change to Madison's proposals, which declared that "no state shall violate the equal rights of conscience, or the freedom of the press, or the trial by jury in criminal cases." Believing, as he did, that the greatest dangers to rights were more likely to arise within the individual states, Madison thought this was "the most valuable amendment on the whole list." But the Senate, as guardians of the legislative authority of the states, thought otherwise.

The amendments approved by the Senate were more compact than the proposals it had received from the House. The most notable change came in the forerunner to the Establishment Clause. The Senate proposed to deny Congress only the power of "establishing articles of faith, or a mode of worship"—a meaningless restriction because American Protestants were already divided into too many denominations ever to be able to reach consensus on such theological matters. This narrow language did not survive the six-member conference committee appointed to reconcile the House and Senate versions. In its final form, the clause took a far more expansive form. Congress would be prohibited from enacting any law merely "respecting an establishment of religion."

After the conference committee completed its work, the two chambers approved the twelve amendments and left it to President Washington to transmit them to the states. Anti-Federalists hardly welcomed the results. None of the structural changes the state conventions had recommended had been approved. The adoption of amendments chiefly concerned with individual rights would atone for the Constitution's great sin of omission, but it would hardly correct its other perceived deficiencies. That disappointment helps explain why the public records relating to the ratification of the amendments are so skimpy, to the deep regret of modern commentators who want to know what Americans really thought about this charter of fundamental rights.

Even so, the amendments made quick initial progress through the states. Had North Carolina and Rhode Island remained outside the Union, nine states would have been required for ratification. When those two states coupled ratification of the Constitution with action on the amendments, the hurdle was raised to ten; and it went one rung higher when Vermont resolved its long-standing territorial dispute with New York and finally joined the Union as the fourteenth state. But as 1790 gave way to 1791 and the nation engaged in its first great constitutional dispute, over Congress's authority to charter a national bank, four states had yet to act conclusively on the amendments: Massachusetts, Connecticut, Virginia, and Georgia. Not until December 1791 did Virginia put the ten amendments that eventually came to be known as the Bill of Rights over the top with the required eleventh vote. Left unratified were the original first and second amendments, relating to the population ratio for the House and congressional pay raises.

Two more amendments followed over the next long decade. The first was occasioned by a sharp reaction against the Supreme Court's decision in *Chisholm v. Georgia*, allowing a sovereign state to be sued by a creditor from another state. The second arose in the wake of the bitterly contested presidential election of 1800–1801, and was designed to cure the constitutional glitch that produced an electoral-vote tie between Thomas Jefferson and his ostensible running mate, Aaron Burr. (Article II originally provided that each elector would cast two votes without distinguishing between the two offices of president and vice president.) With the adoption of the Twelfth Amendment, the amendment process withered. *Proposing* amendments remained easy, of course, for congressmen seeking political notice. But the always formidable odds against *approving* amendments now grew more daunting. The crisis of 1819–1821 over the admission of Missouri as a potential slave state exposed a deep sectional rift between North and South, and inclined many politicians to look for ways to avoid constitutional conflict in the name of preserving national harmony. In the decades leading up to the fateful secession crisis of 1860–1861, an attitude took hold that the Constitution was either too venerable or vulnerable a document to face the stress of amendment by politicians of lesser stature than the Founders.

When the crisis did break in 1860–1861, the lame-duck Thirty-Sixth Congress of the United States entertained a flurry of amendment proposals, all designed to avert catastrophe. With deep and tragic irony, the last proposal to be considered was a self-styled nonamendable amendment to prevent Congress from interfering with slavery in any state where it legally existed. It barely secured the requisite supermajorities in Congress, and went to the states with a tepid endorsement from the new president, Abraham Lincoln, who was still hoping to mobilize Unionist sentiment in the upper South. But the secession movement was too far advanced for the amendment to have any chance of adoption.

On April 12, 1861, the cannons fired on Fort Sumter. And the war came.

The secession of the South was a revolutionary act, not a constitutional one. In a horribly perverse sense, it had more in common with the Declaration of Independence of 1776 than the founding act of the Constitution. Secession marked the attempt of the slaveholding southern states to assume a "separate and equal station among the nations of the earth," not in response to abuses yet committed, but in fearful expectation that a potential northern domination of the national government would somehow put the peculiar institution of human exploitation on which their society rested on the road to extinction. Yet in taking that fateful step of secession, southern leaders did follow one precedent set three-quarters of a century earlier. The secession ordinances were the work of specially elected conventions that mimicked the ratification conventions of 1787–1788 in reverse. Secession would be the work not of ordinary legislators, but of delegates claiming to offer a purer, more direct expression of the sovereign voice of the people.

The end of the war four brutal and bloody years later marked a second founding moment as well—a moment when the Constitution again became a document that the living generation could reshape. Six decades had passed since the last successful amendment. But first the uncertainties of war, and then the promise of emancipation, encouraged some leaders to think that the amendment process could be revived. Wherever Union armies penetrated southern lines, slaves freed themselves by abandoning the plantations of their bondage and seeking refuge and the blessings of liberty with the advancing soldiers. Yet the question of how to eradicate slavery as a legal institution remained something of a puzzle, and Lincoln's Emancipation Proclamation applied only to slaves behind rebel lines. Slowly the idea of using the ultimate legal weapon of a constitutional amendment began to take hold, and much of the credit for its success goes to an unlikely coalition of northern Democrats and abolitionists. The adoption of the Thirteenth Amendment early in 1865 struck the final blow against the cruel system of human domination that had lasted for a quarter-millennium. In proposing it, Congress foresaw that even a constitutional amendment might not make emancipation wholly effective. Section 2 accordingly empowered Congress "to enforce this amendment by appropriate legislation."

Yet members of the Thirty-Ninth Congress elected in 1864 were hardly prepared for the efforts the defeated South quickly launched to salvage the racial hierarchy that slavery once embodied. When they convened in Washington late in 1865, the capital was awash with reports that white-dominated governments in the South were enacting Black Codes designed to reduce the freedmen to a condition of peonage tantamount to slavery in everything but name. To convert the promise of emancipation into a genuine state of legal equality and economic opportunity, Congress enacted the landmark Civil Rights Act of 1866. But because enforcement of this act would plunge the national government into realms of activity previously subject solely to state law, its scope carried well beyond the mere process of emancipation. Many Republicans thought Section 2 of the Thirteenth Amendment gave Congress all the authority it needed. But to resolve any doubts over the federal government's capacity to assume this greatly enhanced role, Congress prepared a further amendment to buttress its constitutional authority.

The result was the Fourteenth Amendment—an omnibus proposal that reversed the Supreme Court's detested decision of 1857 in *Dred Scott v. Sandford* (denying that African Americans, even when free, could ever be vested with the full rights of citizens), laid down new standards of equal citizenship that the states were obliged to honor, and imposed other restrictions on the defeated Confederacy. Ratification of the amendment was the price that southern states had to pay to be readmitted to the councils of national government, meaning that their consent and the constitutional supermajority of three-fourths of the states required for ratification were obtained under duress.

The proper interpretation and application of the Privileges and Immunities, Due Process, and Equal Protection clauses of Section 1 have vexed, challenged, and finally inspired the Supreme Court ever since. At first the Court retreated from giving these clauses a broad application; then, after the turn of the new century, it developed a notion of "substantive due process" that permitted a whole array of state laws, especially those involving the regulation of a modern industrial economy, to be subjected to judicial review. At the same time, the Court—and white Americans in general—agreed that the practices of racial discrimination that the South imposed after the end of Reconstruction were constitutionally permissible under the "separate but equal" doctrine endorsed in its *Plessy v. Ferguson* ruling of 1896. That phrase had appeared in the Declaration of Independence, heralding the new "station" Americans were about to assume "among the nations of the earth." But now it was associated with the inferior station that African Americans were made to occupy within the nation of which they had long been a part. It was not a high point of American jurisprudence—yet the Court's decision in *Plessy* was uncontroversial and reflected a near-consensus of the nation's white citizens.

So the promise of the Fourteenth Amendment long went unfulfilled. Beginning in the 1920s, however, the Supreme Court began to develop the so-called incorporation doctrine, which holds that most (though not quite all) of the rights recognized by the first eight amendments of 1789–1791 apply to the states as well as to the national government. Under the leadership of Chief Justice Earl Warren (1953–1969), the Court used the elastic standards of due process and equal protection to transform the criminal-justice system, engineer the population-based reapportionment of state legislatures and the House of Representatives, and further the great cause of desegregation it began with *Brown v. Board of Education* (1954).

In this quest the Court—and the nation more generally—also united two great legacies of Jefferson and Madison, the Virginia neighbors whom we identify as the leading authors of the Declaration and Constitution (including its original amendments). Jefferson's legacy is written in the language of equality, Madison's in the conception of a national government that might function as a guarantor of rights.

The principle of equality that Jefferson invoked in the preamble to the Declaration had more to do with the equality of peoples than individuals. What he was proclaiming was the right of Americans, in the plural, to exercise their collective right of self-government, rather than the right of each American to enjoy a wholly equal set of liberties. Yet Jefferson—that wealthy spendthrift and slaveowner, the complex personality whose paradoxes trouble us—was also committed to enlightened ideals of individual equality, expressed in his commitment to religious liberty, public education, and a broad distribution of landed property. That was the Jefferson who appealed to later generations of Americans who expanded his famous first self-evident truth of equality to cover individuals as well as peoples. That was the Jefferson, too, to whom Lincoln paid homage in the Gettysburg Address.

The Madison legacy is, characteristically, more nuanced, and bound up with his advanced ideas about the protection of individual rights. In his original view of the late 1780s, Americans needed to learn two basic truths about the protection of rights. One was that the real problem of rights, at least under republican governments, was not to protect the people as a whole against the concentrated power of government. It was, rather, to protect minorities and individuals against "factious" popular majorities whose political will would determine what government would do. The second great truth was that such majorities were more likely to form within smaller communities, including the separate states, than among the shifting diverse interests that would make up the national polity. It followed that the greatest dangers to rights would arise within the individual states, and the best security might come from empowering the national government to limit their unjust actions. That is what the modern expansive interpretation of the Fourteenth Amendment has accomplished. It gives the federal judiciary far greater authority than Madison himself believed it would be able to exercise, but it also does so in ways that are consistent with his original constitutional vision. One reason Madison wanted to give Congress a veto over state laws was that he doubted that federal judges would have the fortitude to oppose their legal views to the political decisions of popularly elected lawmakers. But federal judges and the justices of the Supreme Court have hardly been wallflowers, and their review of state laws and local ordinances often accomplishes the ends Madison had in mind.

Thirteen further amendments have been added to the Constitution since the Fourteenth Amendment was ratified in 1868.* Several of these have had significant effects as well: the Fifteenth, prohibiting the denial of suffrage on the basis of race; the Sixteenth, authorizing income taxes; the Seventeenth, mandating the popular election of senators; and the Nineteenth, extending the vote to women. Yet the idea that the Constitution is a document subject to popular deliberation and serious reconsideration seems beyond the realm of our political imagination. We use the amendment process to enlarge membership in the political community and tinker at the margins with matters like the dates of presidential inauguration or procedures for determining when the president may no longer be able to perform his official duties. But the idea that Article V might be deployed to consider more fundamental questions—such as replacing the Electoral College with a national popular vote—seems like a pipe dream. The Constitution thus seems to remain only an object of interpretation, not true deliberation, which is why we argue so

---

*The most recent, curiously enough, was framed by Madison himself, and was redeemed from two centuries in constitutional limbo by the heroic efforts of a single inspired citizen. See the Twenty-Seventh Amendment, on page 307.

heatedly about the role of courts (and one Supreme Court) in our constitutional structure.

Americans remain a people defined by the ideals of the Declaration and the rules and norms of the Constitution. In our pursuit of the ideal of equality, we have traveled far beyond the notions of the eighteenth century. But in critical respects, our notions of constitutional government remain firmly fixed in the world of the framers of 1787. Perhaps we need to recall Madison's concluding thought in *Federalist* 14: "Is it not the glory of the people of America, that, whilst they have paid a decent regard to the opinions of former times and other nations, they have not suffered a blind veneration for antiquity, for custom, or for names, to overrule the suggestions of their own good sense, the knowledge of their own situation, and the lessons of their own experience?" But when that thought inspires us, we also have to weigh it against another of Madison's observations. "Notwithstanding the success which has attended the revisions of our established forms of government, and which does so much honor to the virtue and intelligence of the people of America," he wrote in *Federalist* 49, "it must be confessed that the experiments are of too ticklish a nature to be unnecessarily multiplied." On the whole, when it comes to these two founding charters, Americans prefer veneration to ticklish experimentation. But as these documents attest, our polity had revolutionary origins.

THE

DECLARATION OF

INDEPENDENCE

THE FINAL congressional deliberations over independence took place over a span of four weeks. On Friday, June 7, 1776, Richard Henry Lee read the resolutions of the Virginia provincial convention, calling for Congress to adopt a declaration of independence, prepare articles of confederation, and solicit "the assistance of foreign powers." After two days of debate (June 8 and 10, with the customary day off to observe the Sabbath), Congress agreed to defer further action on these measures for three weeks. But in the meantime, three committees were set to work on the necessary preparations. The committee to draft a declaration of independence was appointed, with Thomas Jefferson as its chair. The tall, lanky, sandy-red-haired Virginian was only thirty-three, and he had not played a major role in debate since joining Congress a year earlier. Yet he was an admired writer, especially for his 1774 tract, *A Summary View of the Rights of British America*. Jefferson's draft, as revised by the committee he chaired, was ready on June 28. But Congress first needed to debate the substantive question: Had the moment of independence finally come, or should it be delayed still further? Congress discussed that question on Monday, July 1, but put off a final vote until the next day, when the arrival of Caesar Rodney from Delaware and other changes in the membership of the Pennsylvania delegation produced a vote of twelve states for independence. New York still abstained, awaiting fresh instructions from its provincial convention.

July 2 was thus the day that Congress adopted the critical resolution for independence, which is why John Adams expected it to be the date that later generations of Americans would commemorate. The delegates still needed to debate the Declaration itself,

In CONGRESS. July 4, 1776.

The unanimous Declaration of the thirteen united states of America.

which they did, making further changes that Jefferson did not take kindly. The Declaration was approved, of course, on the Fourth — "in the evening," Jefferson recalled, perhaps inaccurately. But a fresh copy still had to be made, and additional copies prepared for transmission to the states. Historians think that most (but not all) of the signatures that adorn the "engrossed" parchment now displayed (and safely secured) in the National Archives were added on August 2.

1. By referring to people rather than provinces, the opening phrases signal that the colonists are now exercising a revolutionary right to fashion a new government, and no longer merely attempting to reclaim the customary rights of their separate provincial legislatures.

"Nature's God" implies a deity giving moral order to the universe, rather than a biblical God of revelation. Over his life, Jefferson developed a nuanced theology of his own, one which regarded the teachings of Jesus as a sublime distillation of moral truths, but which was also profoundly skeptical of the claims of revealed religion, the doctrines of any organized denomination, and, most important, the fundamental Christian belief in the divinity of Jesus.

Since it is the American people who are declaring their independence (not merely Congress), "mankind" indeed means the rest of humanity, who are being informed of the birth of a new political nation.

When in the Course of human events, it becomes necessary for one people to dissolve the political bands which have connected them with another, and to assume among the powers of the earth, the separate and equal station to which the Laws of Nature and of Nature's God entitle them, a decent respect to the opinions of mankind requires that they should declare the causes which impel them to the separation.[1]

We hold these truths to be self-evident, that all men are created equal, that they are endowed by their Creator with certain unalienable Rights, that among these are Life, Liberty and the pursuit of Happiness.—That to secure these rights, Governments are instituted among Men, deriving their just powers from the consent of the governed,—That whenever any Form of Government becomes destructive of these ends, it is the Right of the People to alter or to abolish it, and to institute new Government, laying its foundation on such principles and organizing its powers in such form,

2. "Self-evident" in contemporary usage meant axiomatic, rather than merely obvious. Jefferson originally wrote "sacred & undeniable."

In other contemporary documents, the fundamental natural rights of mankind were more often expressed in language such as that of Article I of the Virginia Declaration of Rights: "the enjoyment of life and liberty, with the means of acquiring and possessing property, and pursuing and obtaining happiness and safety."

The emphasis on the patience with which Americans have borne "a long train of abuses" directly echoes John Locke's analysis "of the Dissolution of Government" in his *Second Treatise of Government,* Chapter 19, Sections 223–225 and 230. Locke did not publish his two treatises until 1689, in the aftermath of the Glorious Revolution that deposed James II. But modern scholarship has conclusively established that Locke wrote this famous tract in the early 1680s, and that it was meant to serve as a manifesto for a revolution yet to occur, not an apology for one that had already taken place. In the eighteenth century, Locke was best known for his *Essay Concerning Human Understanding* and his writings on education, but the clear echoes of the *Second Treatise* in the Declaration indicate that his famous political work had its audience as well.

The "absolute tyranny" George III was accused of establishing was not a royal despotism, but one under which Parliament could theoretically legislate for Americans "in all cases whatsoever," according to the ominous language of its own Declaratory Act of 1766. Yet the Declaration had to make George III the direct object of its indictment because after 1774 allegiance to the crown was the sole and last link connecting the colonies to the realm of Great

as to them shall seem most likely to effect their Safety and Happiness. Prudence, indeed, will dictate that Governments long established should not be changed for light and transient causes; and accordingly all experience hath shown, that mankind are more disposed to suffer, while evils are sufferable, than to right themselves by abolishing the forms to which they are accustomed. But when a long train of abuses and usurpations, pursuing invariably the same Object evinces a design to reduce them under absolute Despotism, it is their right, it is their duty, to throw off such Government, and to provide new Guards for their future security.—Such has been the patient sufferance of these Colonies; and such is now the necessity which constrains them to alter their former Systems of Government. The history of the present King of Great Britain is a history of repeated injuries and usurpations, all having in direct object the establishment of an absolute Tyranny over these States. To prove this, let Facts be submitted to a candid world.[2]

Britain. The resolutions of the First Continental Congress made clear that Americans believed they were not legally subject to the jurisdiction of Parliament, except insofar as they freely consented to allow Parliament to continue to regulate the channels of imperial commerce.

3. Jefferson borrowed the list of charges leveled against the king from the preamble to the constitution he had recently drafted for his own state of Virginia. Rather than begin with the more recent offenses the crown had committed since 1774, he chose to enumerate grievances that Americans had been expressing for decades.

4. The claim that the king could legitimately "suspend" the operations of acts of Parliament was formally renounced in the Declaration of Rights that the new monarchs William and Mary pledged to accept when they ascended to the throne in 1689. The experience of having pending colonial laws routinely vetoed or suspended reminded Americans that their legislatures were denied the status and privileges that Parliament had gained in 1689.

5. In a futile effort to make colonial assemblies more politically manageable, the crown had begun blocking the routine extension of the right of representation to new frontier communities.

6. In 1768 Governor Francis Bernard had moved the Massachusetts General Court from Boston to nearby Cambridge, and in 1774 Governor Thomas Gage convened the assembly even farther away, at Salem.

He has refused his Assent to Laws, the most wholesome and necessary for the public good.[3]

He has forbidden his Governors to pass Laws of immediate and pressing importance, unless suspended in their operation till his Assent should be obtained; and when so suspended, he has utterly neglected to attend to them.[4]

He has refused to pass other Laws for the accommodation of large districts of people, unless those people would relinquish the right of Representation in the Legislature, a right inestimable to them and formidable to tyrants only.[5]

He has called together legislative bodies at places unusual, uncomfortable, and distant from the depository of their public Records, for the sole purpose of fatiguing them into compliance with his measures.[6]

The Declaration of Independence was "engrossed" (or written out in a final fair copy) on parchment for the addition of signatures. The original signed copy is displayed in the National Archives in Washington, D.C. "May it be to the world, what I believe it will be," Jefferson wrote ten days before his death on July 4, 1826, "the signal of arousing men to burst the chains under which monkish ignorance and superstition had persuaded them to bind themselves, and to assume the blessings and security of self-government."

The Revolutionary generation was greatly influenced by the writings of the English philosopher John Locke (1632–1704), whose ideas about epistemology, education, religion, and politics were familiar on both sides of the Atlantic. This is Locke's best-known portrait, done in 1697 by Sir Godfrey Kneller, the German-born artist who was the leading painter at the English court.

7. Royal governors had two ways to deal with unruly colonial legis-latures. They could *prorogue* them—that is, declare an adjournment and set some later date for the lawmakers to reassemble, presum-ably in a better mood. Or they could *dissolve* the legislatures and call fresh elections, in the unlikely hope that voters would come to their senses and elect more pliant representatives.

8. Here Jefferson draws a problematic link between the behavior of royal governors, who could rarely afford to block legislative ses-sions for long periods if they wanted their salaries to be paid, and the behavior of the seventeenth-century monarchs Charles I and James II, who had tried to rule for years at a time without calling Parliament into session.

9. Alarmed over an upsurge of migration from Britain to America in the early 1770s, the British government had actively discussed barring further emigration to the colonies. There is little evidence that any of the measures cited here was actually impairing the set-tlement of North America. Jefferson might also have complained about the practice of sending convicted criminals to the colonies, but Americans were generally content to recruit labor from what-ever sources they could. For his part, Jefferson came to think that migrants from Mediterranean countries would be a useful addition to the population of the South, where they could replace African Americans, whom he wished to see emancipated from slavery but then colonized to other lands. The great magnet for eighteenth-century immigration was Pennsylvania, where the visionary poli-cies of its founder, William Penn, attracted both religious dissent-

He has dissolved Representative Houses repeatedly, for opposing with manly firmness his invasions on the rights of the people.[7]

He has refused for a long time, after such dissolutions, to cause others to be elected; whereby the Legislative powers, incapable of Annihilation, have returned to the People at large for their exercise; the State remaining in the mean time exposed to all the dangers of invasion from without, and convulsions within.[8]

He has endeavoured to prevent the population of these States; for that purpose obstructing the Laws for Naturalization of Foreigners; refusing to pass others to encourage their migration hither, and raising the conditions of new Appropriations of Lands.[9]

He has obstructed the Administration of Justice, by refusing his Assent to Laws for establishing Judiciary powers.

ers and economic-opportunity seekers from the British Isles and Germany. These new groups soon spread out across the middle colonies and into the backcountry of Virginia and the Carolinas.

10. Since 1701, British judges had occupied the bench on condition of good behavior; in America, they still served at the pleasure of the crown. A plan to provide royal salaries to Massachusetts judges sparked a major controversy in that colony in 1772.

11. Americans long complained that successive British ministries were using the colonies as a dumping ground for political patronage, but the idea that the colonies were overrun by "swarms" of hungry or rapacious bureaucrats is fanciful.

12. The presence of several British regiments in Boston in the late 1760s led to the infamous Massacre of March 1770. From June 1774 to March 1776, General Thomas Gage had also relied on British soldiers as he tried (and failed) to execute his commission as governor of Massachusetts.

13. In a general sense, this charge describes the situation of the colonies since the outbreak of war in Massachusetts in April 1775.

14. The "Jurisdiction foreign to our Constitution" refers to Parliament; "pretended Legislation" alludes to all the punitive measures imposed against American rights and interests since the Stamp Act of 1765.

He has made Judges dependent on his Will alone, for the tenure of their offices, and the amount and payment of their salaries.[10]

He has erected a multitude of New Offices, and sent hither swarms of Officers to harrass our people, and eat out their substance.[11]

He has kept among us, in times of peace, Standing Armies, without the Consent of our legislatures.[12]

He has affected to render the Military independent of and superior to the Civil power.[13]

He has combined with others to subject us to a Jurisdiction foreign to our Constitution, and unacknowledged by our Laws; giving his Assent to their Acts of pretended Legislation:[14]

15. The Quartering Acts of 1765 and 1774 authorized military commanders to lodge soldiers in "uninhabited houses, out-houses, barns, or other buildings" as they deemed necessary, "(making a reasonable allowance for the same)," as well as "inns, livery houses, ale-houses, [and] victualling houses."

16. The 1774 Administration of Justice Act allowed British soldiers accused of crimes against Americans to be remanded to Britain for trial. Americans called it the Murdering Act, because they feared it would give Redcoats license to imitate the perpetrators of the Boston Massacre of 1770, in which five colonists were killed.

17. The Prohibitory Act of December 1775 made American ships and goods subject to seizure and confiscation.

18. Americans' original grievance, dating to their resistance to the Stamp Act of 1765 and the Townshend duties of 1767, was that colonists could be taxed only by their own directly elected representatives, not a distant Parliament to which they sent no members.

19. The vice admiralty courts, which enforced the parliamentary Navigation Acts regulating imperial commerce, did not hold jury trials.

20. There is no evidence to sustain this charge, though one Boston seaman was briefly sent to England after being arrested on the charge of urging British soldiers to desert.

For quartering large Bodies of Armed Troops among us:[15]

For protecting them, by a mock Trial, from Punishment for any Murders which they should commit on the Inhabitants of these States:[16]

For cutting off our Trade with all Parts of the World:[17]

For imposing Taxes upon us without our Consent:[18]

For depriving us, in many Cases, of the Benefits of Trial by Jury:[19]

For transporting us beyond Seas to be tried for pretended Offenses:[20]

George III, seen here in the popular coronation portrait by Allan Ramsay, was twenty-two when he took the throne in October 1760. He was educated to be a constitutional monarch, and that meant defending the right of Parliament to legislate for his American colonies. In 1774 Thomas Jefferson offered a simpler definition of his duties: "No longer persevere in sacrificing the rights of one part of the empire to the inordinate desires of another; but deal out to all, equal and impartial justice." The king missed that lesson, and two years later Jefferson addressed him again in harsher terms.

John Trumbull painted many of the signers of the Declaration from life, and Jefferson aided him in the composition of this scene. It was commissioned by Congress in 1817, purchased in 1819, and placed in the U.S. Capitol's rotunda in 1826. Jefferson stands prominently at the center as he presents the Declaration to John Hancock (president of Congress), flanked (from the left) by portly John Adams, Roger Sherman, Robert Livingston, and Benjamin Franklin. The Declaration was submitted to Congress for approval on June 28, 1776. On July 4, after revising Jefferson's draft, Congress adopted it. The delegates affixed their names to the engrossed document over the span of several months.

21. The Quebec Act of August 1774 extended the boundaries of British Canada into the territory west of Pennsylvania and north of the Ohio River, and allowed the province conquered from France to be governed by Parliament, without a representative assembly.

22. This refers primarily to the Massachusetts Government Act of 1774, in which Parliament altered the royal charter of 1691 by making members of the provincial council appointed solely by the crown, and also prohibited town meetings from conducting any business other than the appointment of town officials.

23. "In all cases whatsoever" is the detested formula of the Declaratory Act of 1766, passed to ease the repeal of the Stamp Act through the House of Commons.

24. These two clauses alone could have served as a sufficient justification for independence, since the allegiance Americans owed the king was to be repaid by his protection of their lives and property. Once war erupted in Massachusetts in April 1775, the colonists were morally free to renounce their allegiance to a monarch playing the part of a tyrant. And in fact George III, though hardly a tyrant by the brutal standards of the past century, was perhaps the strongest supporter of his government's policy of military repression of the American revolt. His chief minister, the nervous Lord North, was a far weaker reed whose courage the king regularly had to boost.

For abolishing the free System of English Laws in a neighbouring Province, establishing therein an Arbitrary government, and enlarging its Boundaries so as to render it at once an example and fit instrument for introducing the same absolute rule into these Colonies:[21]

For taking away our Charters, abolishing our most valuable Laws, and altering fundamentally the Forms of our Governments:[22]

For suspending our own Legislatures, and declaring themselves invested with power to legislate for us in all cases whatsoever.[23]

He has abdicated Government here, by declaring us out of his Protection and waging War against us.

He has plundered our seas, ravaged our Coasts, burnt our towns, and destroyed the lives of our people.[24]

25. The news that the king had signed treaties securing the services of mercenary soldiers from the German states of Hesse, Brunswick, and Waldeck convinced many wavering colonists that Britain remained committed to the military suppression of American resistance. As late as April 1776, colonial moderates were eager to hear whether a rumored peace commission would be sent to America to seek an accommodation. The news that the government was instead hiring mercenaries confirmed that there would be no negotiations before a real trial-at-arms had taken place.

26. Captured American seamen generally declined to exchange their imprisonment for service in the royal navy. At the Federal Convention of 1787, Benjamin Franklin cited their dedication as evidence that ownership of property should not be the sole qualification for the right to vote.

27. In November 1775, Lord Dunmore, the governor of Virginia, offered freedom to slaves who would join the British forces.

Jefferson had closed this section of the Declaration with a lengthy and vehement denunciation of the African slave trade, which he described as a "cruel war against human nature." In his account, slavery was not something Americans had ever desired for their own purposes, but a detestable practice that had been forced ("obtruded") upon them almost against their will. Congress deleted this entire passage, not least because the delegates understood it was unseemly to blame the current king for a trade that had begun long before his birth, and in which Americans had freely joined.

He is at this time transporting large Armies of foreign Mercenaries to compleat the works of death, desolation and tyranny, already begun with circumstances of Cruelty & perfidy scarcely paralleled in the most barbarous ages, and totally unworthy the Head of a civilized nation.[25]

He has constrained our fellow Citizens taken Captive on the high Seas to bear Arms against their Country, to become the executioners of their friends and Brethren, or to fall themselves by their Hands.[26]

He has excited domestic insurrections amongst us, and has endeavoured to bring on the inhabitants of our frontiers, the merciless Indian Savages, whose known rule of warfare, is an undistinguished destruction of all ages, sexes and conditions.[27]

In every stage of these Oppressions We have Petitioned for Redress in the most humble terms: Our repeated Petitions have been answered only by repeated injury. A Prince, whose character is thus marked by ev-

28. At this point the Declaration turns from indicting the king to justifying the various acts of protest and resistance that Americans had mounted over the previous decade.

29. The colonists hoped that their protests and the commercial boycott they had initiated in 1774 would mobilize British public opinion to support their cause. In establishing their identity as a separate people and nation, they were severing not only their political connections to the empire, but also their fraternal ties to the British people. In the 1760s, colonial protests against the Stamp Act and the Townshend Duties had generated enough popular support to promote the repeal of those measures. Many Americans believed a similar response in Britain would encourage the government to rethink its decisions. In fact, merchants and artisans worried about the loss of American commerce or sympathetic to the colonists' cause did petition the government for a change of policy. But the ministry of Lord North had called surprise elections in November 1774, and the results effectively insulated the government from popular pressure. This paragraph expresses the disillusionment Americans felt as British policy stuck to its repressive course. To colonial radicals, like Samuel Adams, British policy toward America was the product of ambitious, power-seeking ministers; a tyrannical king; a docile Parliament rotting in political corruption; and a people who once loved liberty, but were now fit for the slavery that would be their fate, too, if the rights of the colonists were suppressed.

ery act which may define a Tyrant, is unfit to be the ruler of a free people.[28]

Nor have We been wanting in attentions to our British brethren. We have warned them from time to time of attempts by their legislature to extend an unwarrantable jurisdiction over us. We have reminded them of the circumstances of our emigration and settlement here. We have appealed to their native justice and magnanimity, and we have conjured them by the ties of our common kindred to disavow these usurpations, which, would inevitably interrupt our connections and correspondence. They too have been deaf to the voice of justice and of consanguinity. We must, therefore, acquiesce in the necessity, which denounces our Separation, and hold them, as we hold the rest of mankind, Enemies in War, in Peace Friends.[29]

30. The appeal to the "Supreme Judge" is again an echo of Locke, who described a legitimate rebellion against tyranny as an "appeal to heaven."

Though we now read the Declaration first and foremost as a statement of the idea of equality among individuals, the intent of this concluding passage—the whole point of the Declaration as a public document and an act of state—was to affirm a different proposition. Americans had become a people and an alliance of provinces entitled to exercise all the powers that other sovereign nations exercised. Having appealed to the "opinions of mankind" to understand the reasons for American resistance, the Declaration ends by asking other states to deal with the United States of America as they did with all other nations.

As important as it was to let the American people know that Congress agreed, with numerous communal and provincial resolutions adopted that spring, that the time to part had come, the Declaration was meant just as much for foreign readers. In that sense, it was a statement of international law, designed to permit and encourage other nations—principally France—to provide the recognition and support the former colonies would require to assure the political independence the document proclaimed.

We, Therefore, the Representatives of the UNITED STATES OF AMERICA, in General Congress, Assembled, appealing to the Supreme Judge of the world for the rectitude of our intentions, do, in the Name, and by Authority of the good People of these Colonies, solemnly publish and declare, That these United Colonies are, and of Right ought to be Free and Independent States; that they are Absolved from all Allegiance to the British crown, and that all political connection between them and the State of Great Britain, is and ought to be totally dissolved; and that as Free and Independent States, they have full Power to levy War, conclude Peace, contract Alliances, establish Commerce, and to do all other Acts and Things which Independent States may of right do.—And for the support of this Declaration, with a firm reliance on the protection of Divine Providence, we mutually pledge to each other our Lives, our Fortunes and our sacred Honor.[30]

Button Gwinnett
Lyman Hall
George Walton

[GEORGIA]

William Hooper
Joseph Hewes
John Penn

[NORTH CAROLINA]

Edward Rutledge
Thomas Heyward, Jr.
Thomas Lynch, Jr.
Arthur Middleton

[SOUTH CAROLINA]

John Hancock

[MASSACHUSETTS]

Samuel Chase
William Paca
Thomas Stone
Charles Carroll of
Carrollton

[MARYLAND]

George Wythe
Richard Henry Lee
Thomas Jefferson
Benjamin Harrison
Thomas Nelson, Jr.
Francis Lightfoot Lee
Carter Braxton

[VIRGINIA]

Robert Morris
Benjamin Rush
Benjamin Franklin
John Morton
George Clymer
James Smith
George Taylor
James Wilson
George Ross
[PENNSYLVANIA]

Caesar Rodney
George Read
Thomas McKean
[DELAWARE]

William Floyd
Philip Livingston
Francis Lewis
Lewis Morris
[NEW YORK]

Richard Stockton
John Witherspoon
Francis Hopkinson
John Hart
Abraham Clark
[NEW JERSEY]

Josiah Bartlett
William Whipple
[NEW HAMPSHIRE]

Samuel Adams
John Adams
Robert Treat Paine
Elbridge Gerry
[MASSACHUSETTS]

Stephen Hopkins
William Ellery
[RHODE ISLAND]

Roger Sherman
Samuel Huntington
William Williams
Oliver Wolcott
[CONNECTICUT]

Matthew Thornton
[NEW HAMPSHIRE]

THE U.S. CONSTITUTION

PERHAPS the most important development in American constitutional thinking to take place in the years 1776–1787 concerned the very idea of a constitution itself. When the colonists began drafting new instruments of government in 1776, they had not yet fully articulated the key definition that has distinguished the American constitutional tradition ever since. This is the idea that a constitution is a written text, adopted by special procedures at a given moment of historical time, which operates as supreme fundamental law by simultaneously empowering but also limiting the institutions of government it establishes. In the revolutionary circumstances of 1776, some leading thinkers at least glimpsed this idea. But the turmoil of war and the novelty of the question prevented the revolutionaries from thinking through the implications of what they were doing. One major problem was that the first constitutions were drafted by the provincial conventions that were also busy acting legislatively. This implied that the constitutions were legally equivalent to statutes—and as such, subject to revision or repeal by any subsequent legislature. As Jefferson later observed in his *Notes on the State of Virginia,* the term "constitution" had different meanings, and simply calling a document a constitution would not make it legally distinct from ordinary legislation.

A critical advance came in Massachusetts, the colony where legal government first effectively collapsed in 1774. In 1775, the Continental Congress authorized the old legislature, the General Court, to resume meeting under the royal charter of 1691, though without the participation of the colony's royal governor, General Thomas Gage. When the General Court later wrote a new constitution to replace the royal charter, Massachusetts towns began

The Federal Convention of 1787 convened in Independence Hall in Philadelphia. The delegates were supposed to assemble on May 14, but spring rains and the usual delays of eighteenth-century travel kept a quorum from gathering until May 25. Here we see the first page of the original parchment copy of the Constitution they drafted over the next four months.

protesting that it was not the right body to undertake this task. Eventually, under political duress, the General Court agreed to call a special convention for the sole purpose of writing a constitution, and to require the convention to submit its work to the consideration of the people of Massachusetts, assembled in their town meetings. Thus was born the two-part process—framing by a special convention, and ratification by the people—that the constitution writers of 1787 also followed. But this innovation was not merely a matter of procedure, for it also embodied the conceptual breakthrough that enabled both supporters and opponents of the Constitution to understand that the document they were debating would truly be the "supreme law of the land."

1. The preamble was significantly revised by the committee of style during the final days of the convention. Instead of referring to the people of the states listed individually, the final wording imagined a single American people exercising their sovereign power, as proclaimed in the Declaration of Independence, "to institute new Government" better designed to protect their essential rights and interests. In the early nineteenth century, the question of whether the formula "We the People" improperly usurped the innate sovereignty of the original states became a heated topic of constitutional dispute and political debate.

2. Read narrowly, the legalistic phrase "herein granted" simply indicates that the national government will possess a specific set of legislative powers. But read broadly, it also illustrates the basic premise of American constitutional thinking. Government does

We the People of the United States, in Order to form a more perfect Union, establish Justice, insure domestic Tranquility, provide for the common defence, promote the general Welfare, and secure the Blessings of Liberty to ourselves and our Posterity, do ordain and establish this Constitution for the United States of America.[1]

ARTICLE I

Section 1. All legislative Powers herein granted shall be vested in a Congress of the United States, which shall consist of a Senate and House of Representatives.[2]

not claim an unlimited or inherent authority to legislate; it wields only such powers as the people entrust to it.

Had the committee of style not deleted a qualifying phrase stating that Congress would "consist of two separate and distinct bodies of men," a constitutional amendment might have been needed to make women eligible for election.

3. Although some of the framers wished to limit suffrage to property owners, there was no practical way to fix one requirement that would effectively cover voters in all the states, or that could anticipate changes in the value of property over time. The clause thus made the basic national and state electorates identical, but states could still impose other qualifications on the right to vote for members of their upper houses or governors.

4. There were no corresponding age requirements mentioned in the state constitutions or specified for election to the British House of Commons. One of the first constitutional questions the House of Representatives faced in 1789 was whether William Loughton Smith, a native of South Carolina, was qualified to represent his state. Smith was studying in England when independence was declared, and returned to Charleston only after the war was over. It could thus be argued, in theory, that he had not yet been a citizen of the United States for seven years. The House rejected this challenge, holding that Smith enjoyed birthright citizenship that his wartime residence overseas did not affect.

By rejecting language requiring "residence" in a state for a fixed period, the framers made newcomers to a state immediately eligi-

Section 2. The House of Representatives shall be composed of Members chosen every second Year by the People of the several States, and the Electors in each State shall have the Qualifications requisite for Electors of the most numerous Branch of the State Legislature.[3]

No person shall be a Representative who shall not have attained to the Age of twenty five Years, and been seven Years a Citizen of the United States, and who shall not, when elected, be an Inhabitant of that State in which he shall be chosen.[4]

ble for election. States cannot add further qualifications for eligibility, and only voters at the polls can limit the number of terms that their elected representatives and (since 1913) senators serve.

5. The precise meaning of "direct Taxes" was uncertain. When Rufus King asked his fellow framers for a definition, Madison recorded that "no one answered." Poll taxes levied on individuals are the clearest example of a direct tax; a flat tax on acreage would be another. In 1796 the Supreme Court addressed the issue in the contrived case of *Hylton v. United States,* the first occasion on which it subjected an act of Congress to constitutional review while upholding a tax on carriages. A century later, in the equally contrived case of *Pollock v. Farmers' Loan and Trust* (1895), the Court struck down a federal income tax as a direct tax requiring apportionment among the states. That question was finally settled by the Sixteenth Amendment.

The three-fifths rule originated in a proposed 1783 amendment to the Articles of Confederation that would have apportioned the common expenses of the Union among the states by population. The use of the phrase "all other Persons" as a euphemism for slaves illustrates the framers' moral embarrassment over having to use the Constitution to recognize slavery as a legally established institution.

Representatives and direct Taxes shall be apportioned among the several States which may be included within this Union, according to their respective Numbers, which shall be determined by adding to the whole Number of free Persons, including those bound to Service for a Term of Years, and excluding Indians not taxed, three fifths of all other Persons.[5]

6. Concern about the mounting difficulty of collecting census data has sparked controversy over whether "actual Enumeration" precludes using statistical sampling procedures that might obtain more accurate results than head-by-head counting. Opponents argue that the framers insisted on accurate headcounts to avoid possible corruption or improper influence in the distribution of seats. Proponents respond that headcounts are more likely to produce errors of omission that significantly disadvantage urban populations and racial and ethnic minorities.

The minimal size of a House district was reduced from 40,000 to 30,000 on the very last day of the Convention, and only then with an unprecedented direct endorsement from George Washington, speaking from the chair, who rightly foresaw that many Americans would be disturbed by the large number of constituents each member of the House would represent. No constitutional requirement limits the size of the House to 435 representatives (as set in 1911), which makes it a smaller body than the British House of Commons.

Unhappiness with the rough estimates used to set the initial allocation of seats helped to convince the framers that a regular census was necessary. Southern delegates wrongly expected future censuses to reveal that their expanding region would move closer to population parity with the North.

The actual Enumeration shall be made within three Years after the first Meeting of the Congress of the United States, and within every subsequent Term of ten Years, in such Manner as they shall by Law direct. The Number of Representatives shall not exceed one for every thirty Thousand, but each State shall have at Least one Representative; and until such enumeration shall be made, the State of New Hampshire shall be entitled to chuse three, Massachusetts eight, Rhode-Island and Providence Plantations one, Connecticut five, New-York six, New Jersey four, Pennsylvania eight, Delaware one, Maryland six, Virginia ten, North Carolina five, South Carolina five, and Georgia three.[6]

When vacancies happen in the Representation from any State, the Executive Authority thereof shall issue Writs of Election to fill such Vacancies.

7. Impeachment is only a power to charge an official with misconduct, and the House thus acts as the equivalent of a grand jury. In seventeenth-century England, impeachment was used as a highly politicized weapon in the recurring struggles between the House of Commons and the Stuart crown. As a hereditary monarch, the king could not be impeached and removed from office (instead, one would either have to charge him with high treason, as when the Puritan revolutionaries tried and executed Charles I in 1649, or rebel against his rule, as happened with James II in 1688). But a monarch's ministers and advisers could be charged for their misdeeds, or as surrogates for grievances against the throne. The use of impeachment for these partisan purposes was abandoned in Britain after 1715. But the American colonial and state legislatures had learned to use impeachment in a less partisan, more prudent way, and the framers drew on their experience.

8. Although states are represented equally, senators vote as individuals, not as members of a delegation. Nineteenth-century state legislatures sometimes issued instructions to their senators, but senators were under no obligation to comply with their recommendations. Senators who declined to do so sometimes resigned their seats, but whether they did so from a sense of political duty or because they now had a convenient excuse to leave Washington is unclear.

9. Because the Senate was regarded as a select advisory council to the president for the special purposes of advising and consenting to major appointments and treaties, it was important to be able to fill vacancies promptly.

The House of Representatives shall chuse their Speaker and other Officers; and shall have the sole Power of Impeachment.[7]

Section 3. The Senate of the United States shall be composed of two Senators from each State, chosen by the Legislature thereof, for six Years; and each Senator shall have one Vote.[8]

Immediately after they shall be assembled in Consequence of the first Election, they shall be divided as equally as may be into three Classes. The Seats of the Senators of the first Class shall be vacated at the Expiration of the second Year, of the second Class at the Expiration of the fourth Year, and of the third Class at the Expiration of the sixth Year, so that one third may be chosen every second Year; and if Vacancies happen by Resignation, or otherwise, during the Recess of the Legislature of any State, the Executive thereof may make temporary Appointments until the next Meeting of the Legislature, which shall then fill such Vacancies.[9]

10. Senators are thus required to have been citizens two years longer than representatives (as specified in Article 1, Section 2). Again, states cannot add further qualifications for eligibility.

11. Why the framers thought a tie vote needed to be broken remains a mystery. In standard parliamentary procedure, a tie, being less than a majority, is ordinarily counted as a defeat. One of many curious errors in the popular 2008 HBO miniseries on the life of John Adams was to have the first vice president cast a tie-breaking vote on the controversial Jay Treaty in 1795, an action that is arithmetically impossible given the constitutional requirement that treaties be ratified by two-thirds of a quorum of the Senate.

12. John Adams and Thomas Jefferson, the first two vice presidents, took their presiding duties quite seriously. Modern vice presidents take the chair only on rare ceremonial occasions, or when their tie-breaking vote might be needed on measures important to the administration.

13. A vice president eager to occupy a higher office might be tempted to issue rulings that would adversely affect an impeached president's defense. At the 1999 impeachment trial of President Bill Clinton, Chief Justice William Rehnquist made a sartorial splash by appearing in the specially striped robes he had begun wearing several years earlier, modeled (informed observers reported) on the costume of the Lord Chancellor in the Gilbert and Sullivan opera *Iolanthe*.

No Person shall be a Senator who shall not have attained to the Age of thirty Years, and been nine Years a Citizen of the United States, and who shall not, when elected, be an Inhabitant of that State for which he shall be chosen.[10]

The Vice President of the United States shall be President of the Senate, but shall have no Vote, unless they be equally divided.[11]

The Senate shall chuse their other Officers, and also a President pro tempore, in the Absence of the Vice President, or when he shall exercise the Office of President of the United States.[12]

The Senate shall have the sole Power to try all Impeachments. When sitting for that Purpose, they shall be on Oath or Affirmation. When the President of the United States is tried, the Chief Justice shall preside: And no Person shall be convicted without the Concurrence of two thirds of the Members present.[13]

14. Anti-Federalists argued that making the Senate the trial court for impeachments violated the strict separation of powers by allowing it to act in a judicial capacity. But as this clause makes clear, the Senate can impose only a political penalty, leaving other punishments for an impeached official to be determined by normal trials at law. Impeachment is first and foremost a political proceeding, not a criminal trial.

15. This clause proved a source of deep controversy during the ratification debates, with Anti-Federalists concocting all kinds of scenarios for its potential misuse. It was first used in 1842 to require all members of the House to be chosen in districts, thereby prohibiting the statewide election of entire delegations, a practice favored by some of the smaller states. In 1873 Congress further required all elections for the House to be held on the Tuesday following the first Monday in November. A 1911 act specified that districts should be "compact and contiguous" in shape, and nearly equal in population, but those provisions were eliminated in a 1929 revision. The increasing urbanization and suburbanization of American society produced enormous disparities in the size of districts drawn by state legislatures dominated by rural members. With the reapportionment revolution of the early 1960s, the Supreme Court required state legislative and congressional districts to be equal in size on the principle of one person, one vote. Madison had foreseen that one potential use of the clause would be to accomplish just that end.

Judgment in Cases of Impeachment shall not extend further than to removal from Office, and disqualification to hold and enjoy any Office of honor, Trust or Profit under the United States: but the Party convicted shall nevertheless be liable and subject to Indictment, Trial, Judgment and Punishment, according to Law.[14]

Section 4. The Times, Places and Manner of holding Elections for Senators and Representatives, shall be prescribed in each State by the Legislature thereof; but the Congress may at any time by Law make or alter such Regulations, except as to the Places of chusing Senators.[15]

16. Prior to the adoption of the Twentieth Amendment in 1933, more than a year elapsed between the election of a new Congress and its first meeting. Until the late nineteenth century, the majority of House members served only one or two terms, indicating either that the republican principle of rotation in office remained something of a political norm; or that state-based political parties wanted to distribute the experience of national service; or that extended service in Washington, D.C., which the British government regarded as a hardship post, was a duty no one could bear too long.

17. In *Powell v. McCormack* (1969), the Supreme Court held that the House could not use its power to judge the qualifications of members to exclude the duly elected though scandal-dogged New York congressman Adam Clayton Powell. It could, however, expel Powell on other grounds, subject to the two-thirds approval required by House rules.

There was no formal quorum requirement in the eighteenth-century House of Commons. In setting one for Congress, the framers worried that members from states closest to the national capital might gain an unfair advantage over those having to travel from more distant parts of the Union.

18. There is a significant formal difference between the rules of each house. The House formally readopts its rules every two years because a fresh election has intervened, affecting all of its members. The Senate acts as a continuing body, because only a third of its seats are contested biennially. The rules of the House enable the majority party to control proceedings effectively; those of the

The Congress shall assemble at least once in every Year, and such Meeting shall be on the first Monday in December, unless they shall by Law appoint a different Day.[16]

Section 5. Each House shall be the Judge of the Elections, Returns and Qualifications of its own Members, and a Majority of each shall constitute a Quorum to do Business; but a smaller Number may adjourn from day to day, and may be authorized to compel the Attendance of absent Members, in such Manner, and under such Penalties as each House may provide.[17]

Each House may determine the Rules of its Proceedings, punish its Members for disorderly Behaviour, and, with the Concurrence of two thirds, expel a Member.[18]

Senate allow the minority and even individual senators to tie up proceedings. The Senate permits unlimited debate on any measure, unless a three-fifths majority (formerly two-thirds under a rule adopted in 1919) approves a cloture resolution to bring it to an end. This "filibuster," as it has been known since the 1850s, once required the windy minority to hold the floor continuously if they wished to prevent action on a measure. Now it is enough that a minority of two-fifths plus one merely signal that they support a filibuster on principle. It has become an open question whether the constitutional norm empowering simple majorities to legislate has thereby been transformed into a procedural rule requiring a supermajority.

As vice president, the ever industrious Thomas Jefferson made a systematic compilation of the Senate's rules, which was published in 1801 as *A Manual of Parliamentary Procedure.*

19. Regular publication of legislative journals was accepted practice in the colonies well before independence, and the galleries were often open to observers. Only in the 1780s did newspapers begin publishing occasional accounts of legislative debates. The debates in the first House of Representatives of 1789–1790 were reported on a daily basis, and public interest in the proceedings ran high. The Senate met in closed session until 1794.

20. Because of its additional functions, the Senate could be called into special session when there was no need for the House to meet, as was the case with the summer 1795 meeting that considered the highly controversial Jay Treaty with Britain. After ratifying it by

Each House shall keep a Journal of its Proceedings, and from time to time publish the same, excepting such Parts as may in their Judgment require Secrecy; and the Yeas and Nays of the Members of either House on any question shall, at the Desire of one fifth of those Present, be entered on the Journal.[19]

Neither House, during the Session of Congress, shall, without the Consent of the other, adjourn for more than three days, nor to any other Place than that in which the two Houses shall be sitting.[20]

the bare two-thirds vote required, the Federalist majority barred publication of the treaty, but a Republican senator defied the ban. The resulting political firestorm led Jay to quip that he could travel cross-country by the light of his burning effigies.

21. At the Convention of 1787, Benjamin Franklin opposed the idea of salaried officials, but most of the framers wanted future representatives to think of public life as a vocation and even career, not an avocation for independently wealthy gentlemen. By providing members with a federal salary, the framers also meant to free them from the improper financial influence of the state governments.

The security against arrest bestowed on legislators derived from English practice, where it protected members of Parliament against intimidation and prosecution by the crown. In the eighteenth century, freedom of speech was still regarded primarily as a right of legislators, not citizens, who could find themselves subject to prosecution for criticizing their representatives too freely.

22. The prohibition against members of Congress simultaneously holding other offices reflects a common belief that the British crown had been using its extensive patronage to corrupt the House of Commons and sap the independence and supremacy that Parliament had gained after the Glorious Revolution of 1688. The Constitution does not explicitly prohibit members of the judiciary from accepting other appointments on behalf of the United States. John Jay was the sitting chief justice when he undertook his special diplomatic mission to England in 1794. Similarly, Associate Justice

Section 6. The Senators and Representatives shall receive a Compensation for their Services, to be ascertained by Law, and paid out of the Treasury of the United States. They shall in all Cases, except Treason, Felony and Breach of the Peace, be privileged from Arrest during their Attendance at the Session of their respective Houses, and in going to and returning from the same; and for any Speech or Debate in either House, they shall not be questioned in any other Place.[21]

No Senator or Representative shall, during the Time for which he was elected, be appointed to any civil Office under the Authority of the United States, which shall have been created, or the Emoluments whereof shall have been encreased during such time; and no Person holding any Office under the United States, shall be a Member of either House during his Continuance in Office.[22]

Robert Jackson served as the leading American prosecutor at the Nuremberg war crimes tribunals after World War II.

23. The original version of this clause, as presented to the convention on July 5, 1787, stated that the Senate could not "alter or amend" revenue and appropriations measures. It was intended as a concession to the large states for the accompanying proposal to give the states "an equal Vote" in the upper house. But Madison and other large-state delegates replied that this was a concession in name only, since the upper house could still reject any measure it disliked.

Americans today might be amused to know that taxes were once commonly regarded as "the free gift of the people." More important, the growing authority of the House of Commons to wield "the power of the purse" was arguably the one "privilege" that best explains the centuries-long development of the broader authority of Parliament. Whatever its other defects, the eighteenth-century House of Commons, and its emulators in the colonial assemblies, knew how to exercise this power quite effectively.

Section 7. All Bills for raising Revenue shall originate in the House of Representatives; but the Senate may propose or concur with Amendments as on other Bills.[23]

Every Bill which shall have passed the House of Representatives and the Senate, shall, before it become a Law, be presented to the President of the United States. If he approve he shall sign it, but if not he shall return it, with his Objections to that House in which it shall have originated, who shall enter the Objections at large on their Journal, and proceed to reconsider it. If after such Reconsideration two thirds of that House shall agree to pass the Bill, it shall be sent, together with the Objections, to the other House, by which it shall likewise be reconsidered, and if approved by two thirds of that House, it shall become a Law. But in all such Cases the Votes of both Houses shall be determined by Yeas and Nays, and the Names of the Persons voting for and against the Bill shall be entered on the Journal of each House respectively. If any Bill shall not be returned by the President within ten days (Sundays excepted) after it shall have been presented to him, the

24. In granting the president a limited negative (or veto) over legislation, this clause took a major step back from the skeptical view of executive power that shaped American thinking in 1776. The crown's abuse of the power to veto or suspend legislation sat atop the list of specific grievances against George III enumerated in the Declaration of Independence. By vesting this power solely in the president, the framers also rejected the Virginia Plan's proposal to give a similar authority to a joint executive-judicial council of revision. Involving judges in the process of lawmaking, they worried, would impair the ability of the judiciary to assess the constitutionality of legislation in properly presented legal cases.

Rather than veto legislation, some modern presidents—notably George W. Bush—have used presidential "signing statements" to express their intention not to enforce duly enacted provisions of legislation they find of doubtful constitutional validity. The requirement of this clause that presidential objections to legislation be formally registered in the congressional journals indicates that the framers would have looked askance at this practice. Indeed, many of them might well be surprised to discover that a president who repeatedly used such statements to justify evading his fundamental obligation to faithfully execute duly enacted laws had not been impeached.

25. One of the most striking developments in modern American governance is the rise of the administrative state comprising countless agencies exercising congressionally delegated power to issue regulations that operate with the force of law. To enforce these regulations, many of these agencies also conduct quasi-

Same shall be a Law, in like Manner as if he had signed it, unless the Congress by their Adjournment prevent its Return in which Case it shall not be a Law.[24]

Every Order, Resolution, or Vote to which the Concurrence of the Senate and House of Representatives may be necessary (except on a question of Adjournment) shall be presented to the President of the United States; and before the Same shall take Effect, shall be approved by him, or being disapproved by him, shall be repassed by two thirds of the Senate and House of Representatives, according to the Rules and Limitations prescribed in the Case of a Bill.[25]

judicial hearings. Beginning in the 1930s, Congress tried to deal with the growth of this administrative state by enabling agency officials to propose and implement new rules that would become effective unless vetoed by resolutions approved by either or both houses. It similarly sought to reserve to itself some capacity to review the quasi-judicial actions that enforcement of regulations entailed. This general practice was challenged in the case of *I.N.S. v. Chadha* (1983). In a 7-to-2 decision, the Supreme Court held that congressional efforts to block administrative actions—whether by a one-house veto or a bicameral veto—were themselves legislative in nature, and thus required approval by both the House and the Senate and submission to the president, who could in turn exercise his veto of a legislative veto.

26. This section embraces most of the formal powers that the Constitution vests in the federal government as a whole, although one critical power—the authority to make treaties with foreign nations, and thus by implication to conduct foreign relations more generally—appears in Article II.

Section 8 consists of a number of individual clauses specifying particular powers. It fittingly begins with one critical power that the Continental Congress never enjoyed: the power to tax. The question of whether the power to provide for the "general Welfare" might enable the national government to assume responsibilities and exercise powers beyond those further identified in this section became an early subject of dispute, first between Anti-Federalists and Federalists, and then between Treasury Secretary Hamilton and Congressman Madison in the early 1790s. Since the New Deal,

Section 8. The Congress shall have Power to lay and collect Taxes, Duties, Imposts and Excises, to pay the Debts and provide for the common Defence and general Welfare of the United States; but all Duties, Imposts and Excises shall be uniform throughout the United States;[26]

the Hamiltonian view that the power can be used broadly has prevailed. The "spending power" allows the national government to make offers of financial support to states and localities that they may simply find too generous and tempting to refuse. No enumerated power gives Congress authority to supervise public education, which Americans have historically regarded as a matter for community and state governance. But the resources Congress has devoted to its support enable the national government to pursue its own policy objectives, most recently through the "No Child Left Behind" legislation.

27. With an adequate power of taxation secured, the national government could draw upon the private wealth of its own citizens and credit markets elsewhere. The most sophisticated eighteenth-century students of political economy understood that Britain's position as the preeminent power of the Atlantic world rested on its capacity to tap the private wealth of its population, not only through excise taxes and duties, but also by appealing to members of the public to lend money to the crown in the expectation of earning interest while fulfilling their patriotic duty. No one understood this better than Alexander Hamilton, the first secretary of the treasury. His brilliant reports on the establishment of public credit remain the greatest state papers in the nation's history.

To borrow Money on the credit of the United States;[27]

28. As a matter of political philosophy, history, and jurisprudence, the spare formula of this clause is freighted with as much significance as any other provision of the Constitution. In the eighteenth century the word "commerce" carried a broad array of associations. It was linked to prevailing ideas of social progress, cultural refinement, and personal politeness, and to the enlightened hope that relations among nations might one day be based on the peaceful exchange of goods rather than military force and diplomatic cunning. But a darker strain of thought also worried that a society immersed in commerce would become soft and effeminate, losing the "manly virtues" that political thinkers since Machiavelli deemed vital to the preservation of republics.

Along with taxation, the need to vest the Union with authority to regulate foreign commerce was one of the two great issues that drove the original movement for constitutional reform in the 1780s. Federalists also understood that removing trade barriers among the states could create a great domestic market that would become an engine of economic growth. States would still compete for economic advantage, but they would do so under the authority of a national government that could promote the free movement of goods, capital, and labor across state lines, and prevent states from erecting barriers to free trade.

Exactly what was meant by "commerce" among the states, however, remained a puzzle. In the leading case of *Gibbons v. Ogden* (1824), Chief Justice John Marshall defined commerce broadly, not as the mere movement and sale of goods but as "intercourse between nations, and parts of nations, in all its branches." His opinion was a high-water mark of nationalist jurisprudence, but its full

To regulate Commerce with foreign Nations, and among the several States, and with the Indian Tribes;[28]

promise took more than a century to realize. By the late nineteenth century, the Supreme Court appeared more intent on setting limits on the regulatory power that Congress had begun to exercise with the Interstate Commerce Act of 1887 and the Sherman Antitrust Act of 1890. Yet as Commerce Clause jurisprudence evolved over the next decades, the Court tacked uncertainly, sometimes accepting the regulatory initiatives Congress was under pressure to adopt, sometimes drawing sharp lines around its power. In *Hammer v. Dagenhart* (1918), for example, the Court overturned a congressional act prohibiting the interstate shipment of goods made with child labor. Under Chief Justice (and former president) William Howard Taft, the Court seemed to broaden the scope of the federal commerce power, but this body of law remained complex and confusing.

The great crisis came when the Court struck down key elements of the first wave of New Deal legislation enacted in 1933–1934 to enable the national government to respond to the Great Depression. Measures like the National Industrial Recovery Act and the Agricultural Adjustment Act regulated prices, hours, wages, and procedures for collective bargaining, and they were adopted under a broad reading of the Commerce Clause. When the Court overturned these and other acts in 1935–1936, it found itself in the politically awkward position of challenging an extremely popular president and strong Democratic majorities in Congress and the electorate, at a moment when the Great Depression was spreading misery across the land. The Court-packing plan that Franklin Roosevelt proposed early in 1937 was only one more round in a continuing struggle that the justices knew they could well lose. The

The Chicago gangster Al Capone, the unlikely benefactor of this Depression-era soup kitchen, made part of his illicit fortune through one constitutional amendment (Prohibition) and went to jail by ignoring another (the income tax). The Great Depression of the 1930s was the gravest domestic challenge the United States faced since the Civil War. It led to a vastly expanded role for the federal government in the regulation of the national economy and the support of a modern welfare state. Yet private charitable activities, like Capone's soup kitchen, retained an important role in the relief of poverty and unemployment.

best evidence suggests that "the switch in time that saved nine" occurred *before* the Court-packing scheme was broached, when Associate Justice Owen Roberts cast his swing vote in conference (the justices' private meeting after oral argument) to uphold a State of Washington statute setting minimum wages. Although the Commerce Clause was not directly implicated in this case (*West Coast Hotel v. Parrish*), Roberts' shift indicated that a majority of the Court was preparing to back down from a continuing confrontation with the political branches. Other decisions involving a second wave of New Deal legislation soon confirmed the fact.

Over the next four years, FDR effectively remade the Court in his own image with the appointment of seven justices. By the early 1940s, a new Commerce Clause jurisprudence had emerged. Now when the Court reviewed economic legislation, it was enough to determine that there was a "substantial relationship" between the activity being regulated (workers' hours or safety, for example) and interstate commerce. That proved an easy test to pass for the highly integrated, complex economy the United States had long since possessed. The Court issued a clear signal of how deferential it was prepared to be in *Wickard v. Filburn* (1942), when it upheld the conviction of a farmer who had planted more wheat than he was allowed to under the revised Agricultural Adjustment Act. Even though all the wheat he harvested was reserved for his own use, farmer Filburn had improperly affected interstate commerce by avoiding buying from a market in which he should have been participating. Tiny actions of individuals, aggregated many times, could have the necessary "substantial effect" on interstate commerce.

Roscoe Filburn was an Ohio farmer who felt he should be able to raise as much wheat as he wished so long as its use was limited to his family and livestock. His 1941 harvest exceeded his allotment under the Agricultural Adjustment Act, and he was fined. Filburn argued that his crop had nothing to do with interstate commerce. The Supreme Court disagreed. Filburn's actions, if multiplied by other farmers, would impair Congress's efforts to maintain adequate prices for wheat growers nationally.

By the mid-twentieth century, then, the Commerce Clause provided the principal basis for the massive federal regulation of the national economy. Under Chief Justice Rehnquist, the Court made several attempts to demonstrate that the Commerce Clause must have some limits. In *United States v. Lopez* (1995) it struck down a federal statute restricting the carrying of firearms near schools as a misapplication of the commerce power. More controversially, in *Morrison v. United States* (2000), it overturned provisions of the Violence against Women Act on similar grounds, even though congressional hearings had established that physical abuse did have a significant impact on women's performance as workers. Conservatives heralded these decisions as signs that the Court would now prove willing to curtail the regulatory power of the federal government. It would be more accurate to conclude that these cases represented distant shots across the bow of Congress that left its enormous economic power largely intact.

The Indian Commerce clause is the basis for the broad authority the national government exercises over Native Americans, whose status, in a famous phrase of Chief Justice John Marshall, is that of "domestic dependent nations," possessed of significant degrees of autonomy yet subject to a government whose authority they never formally or freely ratified. Under the Trade and Intercourse Acts of the 1790s, the new government initiated the practice of negotiating treaties with indigenous peoples, and those treaties were subjected to the same ratification requirement in the Senate (a two-thirds vote) as the one that applied to foreign treaties. Yet the authority for that practice came not from the Treaty Clause proper but from the Indian Commerce Clause.

Chief Justice John Marshall is hailed for his 1803 opinion in *Marbury v. Madison* endorsing the doctrine of judicial review. But many other Marshall Court rulings had a profound impact, including the broad reading of the Interstate Commerce Clause in *Gibbons v. Ogden* and the nuanced interpretation of the Indian Commerce Clause in *Worcester v. Georgia*.

29. Naturalization is the legal process by which a citizen or subject of another nation becomes a citizen of the United States. The original Naturalization Act of 1790 granted this opportunity only to "white persons." One of the striking developments in legal thinking that accompanied the Revolution was the emergence of the idea that citizenship was something that individuals were capable of freely choosing, not merely a legal inheritance determined by the accident of birth or traditional subjection to a monarchical liege.

The inclusion of a bankruptcy provision in the powers of Congress was clearly designed to promote the creation of an integrated national economy. Because the principal object of English bankruptcy legislation was to protect deserving traders against unscrupulous debtors, significant criminal penalties were attached to the enforcement of bankruptcy. Sharing that concern with the interests of merchants, the framers would not have favored a system that enabled debtors to take advantage of diverse state laws to hide recoverable assets from their just creditors. Yet American attitudes toward bankruptcy were already diverging from their English antecedents. Americans were more willing to regard bankruptcy as the result of misfortune as well as personal folly or deceit, and thus were more open to imagining how the law might work to enable debtors to start anew. The first congressional bankruptcy statute of 1800 was short-lived, becoming a casualty of the Republican electoral victory later that year. Subsequent acts were short-term responses to the various panics that regularly wracked the nineteenth-century economy. Not until 1898 did Congress finally enact a permanent bankruptcy statute.

To establish an uniform Rule of Naturalization, and uniform Laws on the subject of Bankruptcies throughout the United States;[29]

30. During the colonial era, Americans dealt with a bewildering array of coins, and specie (hard money) flowed relentlessly across the Atlantic to satisfy the demands of British creditors. Like the power to regulate commerce, the power to coin money and fix weights and measures recognized the benefits of national economic regulation.

31. The reference to "Securities" indicates how much the framers were contemplating a national government that could act as a modern state, issuing instruments of public credit that would allow it to tap the wealth of both its own citizens and foreign investors, and therefore not have to rely on taxation as its sole source of revenue. John Jay, the first chief justice, believed that omission of the modifier "current" could have been construed to prevent the United States from punishing the counterfeiting of foreign coins, such as Mexican dollars, which were a significant part of the circulating money supply in the eighteenth century.

32. From 1810 to 1912, postal regulations kept numerous offices open on Sunday, in part to promote efficiency in the collection and delivery of the mail, but also because closing post offices on that day might be construed as legal recognition of the Christian Sabbath, and thus an offense against the Establishment Clause of the First Amendment.

To coin Money, regulate the Value thereof, and of foreign Coin, and fix the Standard of Weights and Measures;[30]

To provide for the Punishment of counterfeiting the Securities and current Coin of the United States;[31]

To establish Post Offices and post Roads;[32]

33. The sole clause of the original Constitution to bear an explanatory preamble, this provision strikes a balance between the framers' desire to encourage technological innovation and intellectual creativity and their aversion to establishing the kinds of monopolistic and perpetual privileges they associated with the Old World. The use of the specific word "Inventors" indicated that the framers were breaking from English practice, which allowed the benefits of a patent to go to anyone seeking the development of a mechanical innovation, regardless of whether that person was its actual creator in the intellectual or inventive sense. In general, American law proved highly protective of the rights of inventors, but initially showed little interest in extending comparable protection to authors. That attitude toward copyright, however, changed markedly in the twentieth century. Whether "limited Times" means a relatively brief period or a lengthier but still finite one became the subject of an intriguing legal challenge in *Eldred v. Ashcroft,* decided by the Supreme Court in 2003. Under the Sonny Bono Copyright Term Extension Act of 1998, Congress added another twenty years to the existing generous terms. Proponents of the act argued that the extension of the term would give artists and writers additional incentives to create new works. But critics aptly replied that the extension of an existing term could not possibly increase incentives for works already created, and that its real purpose was to secure the very "perpetual privileges" the framers wished to reject. The Court upheld the act. A long congressional tradition of extending both existing and future terms of copyright, it stated, effectively immunized the practice from challenge.

To promote the progress of Science and useful Arts, by securing for limited Times to Authors and Inventors the exclusive Right to their respective Writings and Discoveries;[33]

34. Uncertain whether the new government would need a complete system of courts or could safely rely on the existing state judiciaries, the framers left this fundamental question to the future discretion of Congress. The immediate answer was the Judiciary Act of 1789, written principally by Oliver Ellsworth, a Connecticut lawyer and senator, which remains a landmark of American legislative history, not least for Section 25, which established the right to appeal issues involving federal law and the Constitution from state courts to the Supreme Court. The Judiciary Act provided for two levels of federal courts: district courts in every state, and circuit courts on which justices of the Supreme Court would also sit on panels with district judges. The burden of riding circuit over vast distances soon became a pet grievance of the justices, and in the Judiciary Act of 1801 that duty was eliminated by a lame-duck Federalist Congress as the Republicans were preparing to take power. But the Judiciary Act of 1802 repealed the earlier law and reimposed the burden of circuit riding on the justices, perhaps as a cautionary message to a predominantly Federalist judiciary to respect the results of the recent election that had swept their Republican opponents into office.

35. It therefore falls to Congress, acting legislatively with the consent of the executive or over a presidential veto, to establish rules for detaining, prosecuting, and punishing "enemy combatants," such as modern terrorists whose actions are illegitimate under international law.

To constitute Tribunals inferior to the supreme Court;[34]

To define and punish Piracies and Felonies committed on the high Seas, and Offences against the Law of Nations;[35]

36. In a critical editorial change, the framers substituted "declare" for "make" in the first provision, under the supposition "that 'make' war might be understood as 'conduct' which was an executive function" (as Madison wrote in his notes of the debates for August 17, 1787). The occasions on which Congress has formally declared war have been few, while presidents have frequently committed American forces to combat without requesting or receiving a formal declaration. The major conflicts in Korea (1950–1953) and Vietnam (circa 1964–1973) were waged without such a declaration, though Congress actively consented to those wars by continually renewing appropriations for the military. Under the War Powers Act of 1973, adopted over President Nixon's veto, Congress created a legislative framework empowering presidents to commit American troops to combat for a limited period, subject to subsequent congressional approval. Presidents ever since have argued that this measure represents an improper limitation on their constitutional authority as commander-in-chief of the armed forces and their general responsibility to protect national security. It is generally agreed that the act has proved ineffective. In the Gulf War of 1991 and the Iraq War of 2003, presidents George H. W. Bush and George W. Bush, respectively, intimated that prior congressional approval was not essential to the initiation of hostilities. But both leaders retreated from that position and solicited authorizing congressional resolutions prior to undertaking military action. The framers understood that the president would retain an inherent power "to repel sudden attacks," and it is absurd to imagine that a president would have to wait for Congress to act (or reconvene) before ordering the nation's armed forces to answer an assault in progress. But on occasions

To declare War, grant Letters of Marque and Reprisal, and make Rules concerning Captures on Land and Water;[36]

when a serious threat is perceived in advance and time is available for deliberation, it seems equally wrong to think that presidents can act unilaterally without prior congressional approval. Whether that approval is expressed through a formal declaration of war or a resolution matters less than maintaining the basic principle that our democracy should go to war only when the people's representatives authorize military action.

"Letters of Marque and Reprisal" authorize privateers to capture ships belonging to an enemy nation. Though this clause is now obsolete as a matter of international law, its presence in Article I again illustrates the framers' desire to vest Congress with war-making powers equal to those of the British crown.

37. Beginning in 1689, Parliament adopted the practice of voting "annual supplies" for the military, while prohibiting the king from maintaining "a standing army within the kingdom in time of peace" without its own legal consent. Anti-Federalists argued that the two-year appropriation would encourage Congress to treat the military as a standing army, and, worse, that only with such a despotic force at its disposal would the new government be able to enforce its laws. The idea that standing armies were a danger to liberty was a stock theme of eighteenth-century political rhetoric.

38. Because a navy (as opposed to an army) poses far less of a danger to the rights and liberties of citizens, and because its construction requires greater preparation than that of an army, the Constitution does not limit the duration of naval appropriations.

To raise and support Armies, but no Appropriation of Money to that Use shall be for a longer Term than two Years;[37]

To provide and maintain a Navy;[38]

39. After 1689, Parliament also passed an annual Mutiny Act which evolved into a general-purpose statute authorizing the crown to impose military discipline while also regulating the administration of numerous routine military matters. The king's authority to issue articles of war as the foundation of military justice thus depended on annual legal reauthorization. This clause is the American equivalent of that practice, and another mark of the extent to which the framers were intent on subordinating executive power over the military to legislative authority and supervision.

To make Rules for the Government and Regulation of the land and naval Forces;[39]

40. The Continental Congress had been powerless to assist Massachusetts in suppressing the popular rising of indebted farmers known as Shays's Rebellion, during the winter of 1786–1787. This clause was designed to enable the national government to assist states in resisting either riotous uprisings of their own citizens or slave rebellions in the plantation states of the South.

41. The militia was traditionally regulated by the laws of the colonies, and the legal requirement to serve in it was broadly imposed across the adult male population. But complaints about its performance during the Revolutionary War led the framers to believe that an effective militia required significant national oversight and direction, even while the states would continue to administer the militia and appoint its officers. Anti-Federalists, by contrast, worried that the national government might allow or encourage the state-based militia to atrophy, and then use its own regular army to enforce unpopular or unjust national laws at the point of a bayonet. The resulting debate over the future character and effectiveness of the militia ultimately led to the adoption of the Second Amendment, with its affirmation of the people's right "to keep and bear arms." Maintaining an adequately armed militia was a matter of special concern in the South, where the existing fear of slave rebellion was compounded by British efforts to entice slaves to leave their masters and seek refuge behind "enemy" lines.

To provide for calling forth the Militia to execute the Laws of the Union, suppress Insurrections and repel Invasions;[40]

To provide for organizing, arming, and disciplining, the Militia, and for governing such Part of them as may be employed in the Service of the United States, reserving to the States respectively, the Appointment of the Officers, and the Authority of training the Militia according to the discipline prescribed by Congress;[41]

42. In June 1783 a clamorous group of unpaid Continental soldiers besieged the Continental Congress during its sessions at the Pennsylvania Statehouse in Philadelphia. After state authorities refused to call out the militia for its protection, Congress adjourned to Princeton. Over the next two years Congress migrated from there to Annapolis and Trenton before finally settling in New York City. Although adoption of this clause would not prevent the new government from remaining in New York or relocating to Philadelphia, it opened the possibility of founding a completely new capital. As part of the famous Compromise of 1790, congressman James Madison relaxed his opposition to Treasury Secretary Hamilton's plan for the national assumption of state debts. In return, key Hamilton supporters agreed that the government would return to Philadelphia for the near future, until a permanent capital could be constructed along the Potomac River on swampy land provided by Virginia and Maryland.

43. Anti-Federalists called this the "sweeping clause." They worried that it gave Congress virtually unlimited authority to legislate and would thus circumvent the delegation of specific powers in the immediately preceding clauses. Federalists replied that it was simply a way of ensuring that Congress would have the discretionary authority to carry out its assigned duties. The most important debate over the clause took place in 1791, when Madison and Secretary of State Jefferson urged President Washington to veto a bill creating a national bank on the grounds that Congress lacked the explicit authority to issue charters of incorporation. The president instead accepted the judgment of Hamilton, who relied on a broad

To exercise exclusive Legislation in all Cases whatsoever, over such District (not exceeding ten Miles square) as may, by Cession of particular States, and the Acceptance of Congress, become the Seat of the Government of the United States, and to exercise like Authority over all Places purchased by the Consent of the Legislature of the State in which the Same shall be, for the Erection of Forts, Magazines, Arsenals, Dock-Yards, and other needful Buildings;—And[42]

To make all Laws which shall be necessary and proper for carrying into Execution the foregoing Powers, and all other Powers vested by this Constitution in the Government of the United States, or in any Department or Officer thereof.[43]

interpretation of this "Necessary and Proper" Clause. In the famous case of *McCulloch v. Maryland* (1819), Chief Justice John Marshall again relied on a Hamiltonian construction of "necessary and proper" while upholding the constitutionality of the federal charter establishing the Second Bank of the United States. Marshall deemed this matter so urgent that he pseudonymously published a series of newspaper essays justifying his opinion for the Court while rebutting the criticisms leveled against it by Spencer Roane, the leading Virginia jurist who was Marshall's chief critic and legal nemesis.

44. The phrase "such Persons" is once again a euphemism for slaves. The Convention's decision to allow new importations for a period of two decades was a concession to South Carolina and Georgia. In the upper South there was no perceived need to renew the slave trade because the dominant planter class knew that African American slaves were already a demographically self-reproducing population. Congress exercised its power as soon as it was permitted to do so, and the importation of African slaves effectively ended in 1808 (though some smuggling doubtless continued). It was not illegal migration from Africa that shaped the future of American slavery, however, but the domestic trade that carried large numbers of African Americans from the Upper South to the fertile lands of the Cotton Belt, which ultimately stretched from Georgia into Texas. That domestic slave trade, in turn, is what made this clause deeply controversial during the Missouri Crisis of 1819–1821, when opponents of slavery argued that Congress could now prohibit the migration of slaves from one state

Section 9. The Migration or Importation of such Persons as any of the States now existing shall think proper to admit, shall not be prohibited by the Congress prior to the Year one thousand eight hundred and eight, but a Tax or duty may be imposed on such Importation, not exceeding ten dollars for each Person.[44]

to another. Southern leaders (including Madison, recently retired from the presidency) argued that the use of the word "migration" was never meant to cover movement across state lines, and indeed it is difficult to see why their states would have accepted such a prohibition in 1788. But basic rules of interpretation hold that the words of a constitutional text cannot be redundant. If "importation" is also separately barred, "migration" must refer to something else—and that could hardly be a reference to movement *within* a state.

45. The placement of this clause within Article I implies that this "Great Writ" protecting citizens against arbitrary arrest and confinement can be suspended only by Congress. In Latin, *habeas corpus* literally means, "that you have the body," but the legal meaning of the writ is that an officer of state is being commanded to physically produce a person under detention or imprisonment, as part of a judicial proceeding to ascertain whether that individual's loss of liberty is legally justifiable. President Lincoln effectively challenged that monopoly in 1861, denying *habeas corpus* to suspected Confederate sympathizers before Congress convened in special session to deal with the outbreak of civil war. In doing so, he also ignored a legal challenge from Chief Justice Roger Taney. Lincoln's action recognizes the possibility that, under emergency conditions, the president may have to act unilaterally in the expectation that Congress or the courts will subsequently legitimate his decision. Lincoln asked Congress to approve his actions retrospectively, and it eventually complied.

The Privilege of the Writ of Habeas Corpus shall not be suspended, unless when in Cases of Rebellion or Invasion the public Safety may require it.[45]

46. A "bill of attainder" historically referred to acts of Parliament accusing named individuals of treason, and levying punishment of death and confiscation of property.

An *ex post facto* law criminalizes or imposes penalties upon behavior after the act in question has already occurred.

47. This was a political concession to the South, the region which in the eighteenth century produced the nation's most valuable agricultural exports: tobacco from the Chesapeake colonies (Virginia, Maryland), rice and indigo from South Carolina. A tax imposed on products cultivated by slave labor might ultimately operate as a tax on slavery itself, if it made those commodities more expensive and thus less competitive on foreign markets.

48. These two clauses reflect one of the recurring concerns of any federal system that governs a geographically diverse nation: How does one limit the extent to which some policies might be inevitably perceived to favor one region or locale over another? So far as maritime commerce was concerned, the market, not the government, would determine the channels of trade.

No Bill of Attainder or ex post facto Law shall be passed.[46]

No Capitation, or other direct, Tax shall be laid, unless in Proportion to the Census or Enumeration herein before directed to be taken.

No Tax or Duty shall be laid on Articles exported from any State.[47]

No Preference shall be given by any Regulation of Commerce or Revenue to the Ports of one State over those of another: nor shall Vessels bound to, or from, one State, be obliged to enter, clear, or pay Duties in another.[48]

49. This clause again affirms that the power of the purse is vested solely in the people's elected representatives, and that the people have a right to know how their taxes are being spent.

50. Eighteenth-century Americans were proudly republican in their political convictions, and to be a republican meant renouncing the principle of aristocratic rank and hereditary titles. In 1789 Vice President John Adams provoked a minor flap simply by proposing that the president be formally addressed as "His High Mightiness." Perhaps the portly vice president could be addressed as "His Rotundity," wags scoffed.

51. The prohibitions relating to coinage, bills of credit, legal tender, and "the Obligation of Contracts" express the framers' fears that popular majorities in the states would pass laws adversely affecting the just rights of creditors. Amid the economic troubles of the mid-1780s, popular cries for debtor and tax relief alarmed many of the propertied and creditor interests, who soon formed a natural constituency for the constitutional reforms of 1787. If the state legislatures responded to these appeals, vested property rights would become insecure and creditors would have to run away from debtors eager to pay them with depreciated paper money. Few were more alarmed by these populist tendencies than Madison, who would have preferred giving Congress the power to veto the kinds of state laws that would produce these forms of injustice.

No Money shall be drawn from the Treasury, but in Consequence of Appropriations made by Law; and a regular Statement and Account of the Receipts and Expenditures of all public Money shall be published from time to time.[49]

No Title of Nobility shall be granted by the United States: And no Person holding any Office of Profit or Trust under them, shall, without the Consent of the Congress, accept of any present, Emolument, Office, or Title, of any kind whatever, from any King, Prince, or foreign State.[50]

Section 10. No State shall enter into any Treaty, Alliance, or Confederation; grant Letters of Marque and Reprisal; coin Money; emit Bills of Credit; make any Thing but gold and silver Coin a Tender in Payment of Debts; pass any Bill of Attainder, ex post facto Law, or Law impairing the Obligation of Contracts, or grant any Title of Nobility.[51]

52. In adopting this clause, the framers were concerned that individual states might levy duties on commodities produced in other states or adopt protectionist policies to benefit local manufacturers over competitors in other states or foreign nations. Either use could lead to the erection of barriers against the free flow of goods across state lines, and thus impede the creation of a genuine national market. It would also give an unfair advantage to states which would receive the initial importation of goods from overseas that were destined for consumption elsewhere: they could enhance their own revenues with duties that consumers in other states would ultimately pay. The application of the phrase "absolutely necessary" to the provision permitting fees to be imposed for the valid purpose of administering "inspection laws" protective of the health of residents or local agricultural produce illustrates the deep suspicion with which the framers viewed the self-interested motives of the states. The final clause, asserting a residual congressional authority over "all such Laws," reflects the same concern.

53. The general tenor of this clause suggests that the framers were principally concerned with state acts or interstate agreements that would adversely affect national security interests. But the use of the open-ended phrase "any Agreement or Compact" implies that other interstate agreements that detract from the authority of the national government are also suspect.

One currently pending proposal for a novel interstate compact is the so-called National Popular Vote, which is designed to replace the existing mode of selecting the president by state-based elec-

No State shall, without the Consent of the Congress, lay any Imposts or Duties on Imports or Exports, except what may be absolutely necessary for executing its inspection Laws: and the net Produce of all Duties and Imposts, laid by any State on Imports or Exports, shall be for the Use of the Treasury of the United States; and all such Laws shall be subject to the Revision and Controul of the Congress.[52]

No State shall, without the Consent of Congress, lay any Duty of Tonnage, keep Troops, or Ships of War in time of Peace, enter into any Agreement or Compact with another State, or with a foreign Power, or engage in War, unless actually invaded, or in such imminent Danger as will not admit of delay.[53]

tions without resorting to the difficult requirements for constitutional amendments. Under this scheme, a coalition of states with a majority of presidential electors would agree to bind their electoral votes to whichever candidate carries the national popular vote, regardless of the preferences of their own citizens. Proponents argue that this can be done by an interstate compact that would not require congressional approval. Critics reply that any proposal affecting an issue as momentous as presidential election is clearly a matter of national and constitutional concern, and neither could nor should be kept from congressional scrutiny.

Howard Chandler Christie's famous *Scene at the Signing of the Constitution of the United States* (painted in 1940) represents the signing of the Constitution on September 17, 1787, as a singular triumphal moment in the forging of the federal Union. Yet months of public debate and political maneuvering were still required to turn the proposed Constitution into an agreement binding the states and the "American people" whose national existence the Preamble proclaimed. In many ways the debate that took place "out-of-doors" over the next year was as remarkable as the deliberations at the State House. Christie's painting now hangs in the east grand stairway in the House of Representatives wing of the Capitol.

54. The meaning of this simple declaratory sentence has been controversial since at least 1793, when Alexander Hamilton first noted the difference between the formulas used to vest legislative power in Congress and those vesting executive power in the president. Whereas Article I referred to the "legislative Powers herein granted," the Vesting Clause of Article II simply spoke of "the executive Power." The implication was that there was some inherent executive power that the Constitution was vesting intact in the president, and that particular powers mentioned later in Article II were merely examples or specifications of that general grant of executive authority. Writing pseudonymously as "Pacificus," Hamilton used this distinction while justifying President Washington's unilateral decision, taken without consulting either Congress or the Senate, to issue a proclamation of neutrality in the war between revolutionary France and counter-revolutionary Britain. Criticizing this position, James Madison (writing as "Helvidius") argued that Hamilton (there was no doubt as to his identity) was relying on a definition of executive power more consistent with the royal prerogative of Britain than with the republican principles of the Constitution. Their dispute remains fundamental to the ongoing controversy over the scope of executive power in matters of war and diplomacy.

It is also fundamental to the "unitary executive theory," which holds that the president, as sole repository of executive power, possesses a commanding authority that permeates the entire executive branch. One application of this theory, for example, objects that the appointment of independent counsel to prosecute politically sensitive allegations of executive-branch misconduct is not

ARTICLE II

Section 1. The executive Power shall be vested in a President of the United States of America.[54]

only bad policy (because the resulting investigations can go on endlessly, expensively, and fruitlessly) but constitutionally impermissible (because such counsel are not subject to presidential supervision, as the Vesting Clause, coupled with the president's duty to "take Care that the Laws be faithfully executed," could require). An even stronger version of the theory makes the existence of independent regulatory agencies constitutionally suspect.

55. With the exception of the governor of New York, all of the state executives in the 1780s were appointed annually, bringing the most dangerous branch of government into conformity with the republican maxim, "Where annual election ends, slavery begins." A four-year term for the presidency thus marked a radical break with that principle, indicating how much the framers wanted to turn the executive into an active force within government.

56. Though presidential electors have long been chosen by popular vote in every state, the constitutional right to determine how electors are to be appointed is vested in the state legislatures. Strictly speaking, Americans have no constitutional right to vote for the highest elective office in the land.

Partisan manipulation of the rules for appointing electors was a major factor in the presidential election of 1800–1801, which is usually remembered for the electoral tie between Jefferson and his running mate, Aaron Burr. Republican-dominated Virginia abandoned its district scheme, used in the election of 1796, for a winner-take-all statewide selection. In response, Federalist-controlled Massachusetts scrapped its district system for an appointment by

He shall hold his Office during the Term of four Years, and, together with the Vice President, chosen for the same Term, be elected as follows:[55]

Each State shall appoint, in such Manner as the Legislature thereof may direct, a Number of Electors, equal to the whole Number of Senators and Representatives to which the State may be entitled in the Congress: but no Senator or Representative, or Person holding an Office of Trust or Profit under the United States, shall be appointed an Elector.[56]

the legislature. In New York, Alexander Hamilton urged Governor John Jay to reconvene a lame-duck Federalist assembly to substitute election by districts for the existing rule of appointment by the new legislature that Republicans would dominate, thanks to Burr's brilliant efforts to turn out the vote in New York City. Jay ignored Hamilton's suggestion, which he docketed as "a measure for party purposes wh[ich] I think it w[oul]d not become me to adopt." Pennsylvania nearly sat the election out while the Federalist senate and Republican house haggled over the issue.

It is sometimes argued that the Republican victory of 1800 depended on the use of the three-fifths rule for allocating presidential electors as well as members of the House. Had the rule not inflated the South's share of electoral votes, Jefferson and Burr might not have gained their national majority. The implication appears to be that honest John Adams was still the people's choice, while Jefferson profited yet again from his connections to slavery. But this interpretation ignores the various ways in which states manipulated electoral rules for partisan advantage, or in which the appointment of electors by Federalist legislatures was belied by the popular vote for representatives. New Jersey, for example, cast seven electoral votes for Adams but elected five Republicans to the House. Rhode Island similarly added four electors to Adams' column but gave its two House seats to Republicans. Had Pennsylvania's electors been chosen by the people, not the legislature, Jefferson and Burr would have done better than the 8–7 electoral-vote split negotiated by a Federalist state senate and Republican lower house.

The Electors shall meet in their respective States, and vote by Ballot for two Persons, of whom one at least shall not be an Inhabitant of the same State with themselves. And they shall make a List of all the Persons voted for, and of the Number of Votes for each; which List they shall sign and certify, and transmit sealed to the Seat of the Government of the United States, directed to the President of the Senate. The President of the Senate shall, in the Presence of the Senate and House of Representatives, open all the Certificates, and the Votes shall then be counted. The Person having the greatest Number of Votes shall be the President, if such Number be a Majority of the whole Number of Electors appointed; and if there be more than one who have such Majority, and have an equal Number of Votes, then the House of Representatives shall immediately chuse by Ballot one of them for President; and if no Person have a Majority, then from the five highest on the List the said House shall in like Manner chuse the President. But in chusing the President, the Votes shall be taken by States, the Representation from each State having one Vote; A quorum for this Purpose shall

57. Rather than forming a true Electoral College—a term not used in 1787—or a body like the College of Cardinals of the Roman Catholic Church, the electors vote on separate state campuses and never assemble to deliberate collectively.

Expecting that electors would naturally prefer candidates from their own states, the framers hoped that the rule requiring that one ballot be cast for an "Inhabitant" of another state would encourage them to think in national rather than parochial terms. Electors' first votes were likely to go for "favorite sons," as they used to be called; but everyone's second choice, Madison observed in a nice game-theoretical insight, would be the collective first. Many of the framers expected the electoral system to operate more like a nominating caucus, identifying a set of leading candidates from whom the House would make the final selection. The Twelfth Amendment radically altered these procedures.

58. Under an act of 1792, electors had to be appointed within thirty-four days of the date on which they had to assemble to cast their votes. The change to the Tuesday following the first Monday in November was prompted by a Cincinnati congressman, Alexander "Bully" Duncan, who alleged that Whig voters from Kentucky had crossed the Ohio River to vote in his state, contributing to his own defeat in the famous Log Cabin, "Tippecanoe and Tyler Too" election of 1840. Requiring that all electors be appointed on the *same day* would significantly reduce the ability of voters to appear in two states. Duncan wanted both presidential electors and congressional representatives to be chosen on the same day, but Congress

consist of a Member or Members from two thirds of the States, and a Majority of all the States shall be necessary to a Choice. In every Case, after the Choice of the President, the Person having the greatest Number of Votes of the Electors shall be the Vice President. But if there should remain two or more who have equal Votes, the Senate shall chuse from them by Ballot the Vice President.[57]

The Congress may determine the Time of chusing the Electors, and the Day on which they shall give their Votes; which Day shall be the same throughout the United States.[58]

initially applied the rule only to the electors, and did not national-
ize the day for electing representatives until 1873.

59. Whimsical law professors take special pleasure in this clause.
Might it disqualify a citizen born by caesarean section? How about
those born abroad whose parents are American citizens, such as
George Romney (a candidate in 1968) or John McCain (Republican
nominee in 2008)? The Naturalization Act of 1790 declared that
children born abroad of American citizens were citizens themselves, but even a contemporaneous statute declaratory of the
meaning of the Constitution cannot be perfectly equated with the
Constitution itself.

Perhaps the "natural born" requirement violates Americans'
deep commitment to the principle of equal opportunity by denying foreign-born citizens the opportunity to serve as president. Yet
it should be remembered that the executive is unique in vesting
the whole power of an entire department in a single person. It was
not nativist prejudice but simple prudence that led the framers to
worry that a single individual might be vulnerable to foreign bribes
and influence, or a simple partiality to his native land. Nor was the
clause written to exclude Alexander Hamilton from the presidency,
as a constitutional urban legend would have it. As a native subject
of the British crown, he did not have to be naturalized, and was
clearly a citizen when the Constitution was adopted.

No Person except a natural born Citizen, or a Citizen of the United States, at the time of the Adoption of this Constitution, shall be eligible to the Office of President; neither shall any Person be eligible to that Office who shall not have attained to the Age of thirty five Years, and been fourteen Years a Resident within the United States.[59]

60. The delicate question of exactly how a president's "Inability to discharge the Powers and Duties" of office would be determined was left unresolved until the adoption of the Twenty-Fifth Amendment in 1967. In 1919 a major stroke effectively debilitated President Woodrow Wilson, yet no transfer of power took place to Vice President Thomas Marshall. Similarly, in 1956 President Dwight Eisenhower was hospitalized with a major heart attack, but Vice President Richard Nixon did not act as president in his place.

61. Prior to the Revolution, payment of the salaries of royal governors had been a recurring source of political dispute between the colonial legislatures and the British crown. As appointees of the crown, the governors were often instructed to seek permanent salaries from the legislatures. But the legislatures found the control of salaries too handy a weapon to yield willingly. An executive whose salary was set by the people's representatives would think twice, the argument ran, about violating the people's rights and liberties. In these struggles, the governors usually blinked first. In 1771 the crown's decision to pay the salary of Governor Thomas Hutchinson of Massachusetts from the king's own civil list became one of the grievances that helped make the Bay Colony a potential tinderbox of resistance to imperial policies.

In Case of the Removal of the President from Office, or of his Death, Resignation, or Inability to discharge the Powers and Duties of the said Office, the Same shall devolve on the Vice President, and the Congress may by Law provide for the Case of Removal, Death, Resignation or Inability, both of the President and Vice President, declaring what Officer shall then act as President, and such Officer shall act accordingly, until the Disability be removed, or a President shall be elected.[60]

The President shall, at stated Times, receive for his Services, a Compensation, which shall neither be encreased nor diminished during the Period for which he shall have been elected, and he shall not receive within that Period any other Emolument from the United States, or any of them.[61]

62. Contrary to popular legend, there is no contemporary evidence that George Washington spontaneously added the phrase "So help me God" at his inauguration in 1789. At the 2009 inauguration ceremony, Chief Justice John Roberts mangled the oath by dangling the adverb "faithfully" out of its assigned place, and a seemingly bemused President Barack Obama did not have the heart to correct him. To be on the safe side, Obama took the oath again the next day.

63. The Commander-in-Chief Clause operates, first and foremost, to affirm the fundamental principle of civilian supremacy over the military. But it also illustrates the extent to which, in the realm of national security, the Constitution is "an invitation to struggle." Numerous clauses of Article I exemplify the framers' deep commitment to the idea that military affairs are a matter for close legislative regulation. The authority of Congress to declare war can also be read broadly to suggest that any decision to initiate hostilities requires its prior approval. Yet there are many occasions when the use of armed force must be undertaken urgently, or where it will not lead the nation into war—or, alternatively, where the president's ability simply to deploy military and naval forces may create situations that could make war more likely. U.S. naval operations in the Gulf of Tonkin in August 1964 are a famous and still controversial example of the last.

President George W. Bush frequently invoked his authority as commander-in-chief to argue that neither Congress nor the federal judiciary could actively monitor or regulate his conduct of the global "war on terror" that began after the attacks of September 11,

Before he enter on the Execution of his Office, he shall take the following Oath or Affirmation:—"I do solemnly swear (or affirm) that I will faithfully execute the Office of President of the United States, and will to the best of my Ability, preserve, protect and defend the Constitution of the United States."[62]

Section 2. The President shall be Commander in Chief of the Army and Navy of the United States, and of the Militia of the several States, when called into the actual Service of the United States; he may require the Opinion, in writing, of the principal Officer in each of the executive Departments, upon any Subject relating to the Duties of their respective Offices, and he shall have Power to grant Reprieves and Pardons for Offences against the United States, except in Cases of Impeachment.[63]

2001. That claim met substantial resistance, first from the federal judiciary, then from Congress, but only after the opposition Democratic Party regained control of both houses in 2006.

The fact that the Constitution explicitly gives the president the trifling authority to require his chief subordinates to report in writing illustrates the uncertainty with which the framers thought about executive power more generally. No one in 1789 could easily have said whether the president would become the dominant active force within an administration, or literally serve as a presiding officer supervising a set of ministers with some autonomy of their own. Indeed, this whole sentence is a curious grab-bag of three quite distinct powers that have no obvious relation to one another.

64. Well into August 1787, the framers assumed that the treaty- and appointment-making powers would be vested in the Senate. Only in the September 4 report of the Committee on Postponed Parts were these duties shifted to the president, to act with the "Advice and Consent of the Senate." With its original appointment by the state legislatures and the equal state vote, the Senate bore some resemblance to the discredited Continental Congress, which twice had plunged into months of factional wrangling over issues of foreign policy. Anti-Federalists subsequently argued that these links violated the separation of powers by making the Senate too much a part of critical executive functions. They also evoked nightmarish scenarios in which two-thirds of a bare quorum of senators might

He shall have Power, by and with the Advice and Consent of the Senate, to make Treaties, provided two thirds of the Senators present concur; and he shall nominate, and by and with the Advice and Consent of the Senate, shall appoint Ambassadors, other public Ministers and Consuls, Judges of the supreme Court, and all other Officers of the United States, whose Appointments are not herein otherwise provided for, and which shall be established by Law: but the Congress may by Law vest the Appointment of such inferior Officers, as they think proper, in the President alone, in the Courts of Law, or in the Heads of Departments.[64]

gather by stealth to approve a treaty of special benefit to their own states.

George Washington originally read the "advice" requirement quite literally. The first time the negotiation of a treaty was pending (in this case, with various Indian tribes of the Southeast), he attended the Senate personally in expectation of discussing the matter jointly. The senators found his presence somewhat disconcerting, and some wanted to discuss the matter first in committee. Eventually Washington withdrew, "with a discontented air." He returned the following Monday, however, suggesting that he still thought of the Senate as a council whose advice he might take directly. The practice of direct personal consultation soon lapsed.

65. Practice has seemingly transformed the apparent meaning of this clause. Instead of allowing the president to make appointments to offices that become vacant during a Senate recess, it allows presidents to make interim appointments whenever the Senate is in recess, regardless of how brief that recess might be (say, a holiday weekend) or exactly when the office to be filled was vacated. Presidents have used this power to make interim appointments of nominees whom the Senate has refused to confirm or whose confirmation seems highly unlikely.

66. This section best defines the framers' conceptions of the domestic responsibilities of the president. The presidential veto over legislation (established in Article I) effectively makes the presidency a branch of Congress, and the authority to propose "Measures" for "their Consideration" further implies that an adminis-

The President shall have Power to fill up all Vacancies that may happen during the Recess of the Senate, by granting Commissions which shall expire at the End of their next Session.[65]

Section 3. He shall from time to time give to the Congress Information of the State of the Union, and recommend to their Consideration such Measures as he shall judge necessary and expedient; he may, on extraordinary Occasions, convene both Houses, or either of them, and in Case of Disagreement between them, with Respect to the Time of Adjournment, he may adjourn them to such Time as he shall think proper; he shall receive Ambassadors and other public Ministers; he shall take Care that the Laws be faithfully executed, and shall Commission all the Officers of the United States.[66]

tration can actively promote its own legislative program, and not simply inform legislators returning to the capital what has happened in their absence. The most ambitious presidents use this authority, as well as the enormous resources of the executive branch, to shape and even control the congressional agenda. Yet a well-known adage reminds us that "the president proposes, and Congress disposes."

The power to "receive Ambassadors and other public Ministers" quickly evolved into a substantive power to determine whether the United States recognizes the legitimacy of the governments these envoys represented. This is a critical matter when a revolutionary regime has displaced its legal predecessor. The clause first became controversial in 1793, with the arrival of *Citoyen* Edmond-Charles Genêt as the official envoy from revolutionary France.

The president's responsibility to oversee the faithful execution of the laws embodies a core value of republican government, yet the Constitution treats this basic duty almost as an afterthought. The fact that laws can be enacted over a presidential veto might imply that the president is obliged to execute measures whose constitutionality he continues to doubt, on the grounds that the collective supermajoritarian judgment of both houses of Congress outweighs the scruples of a single official. On the other hand, the language of the presidential oath might be read to create a set of overriding obligations to the Constitution that a conscientiously sworn official must honor according to his or her own judgment.

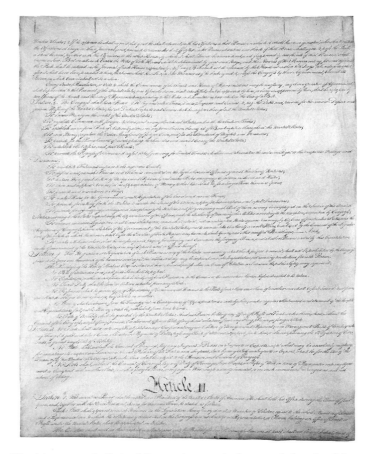

The delegates to the Federal Convention met six days a week from late May to mid-September 1787. The spare language of the final text of the Constitution barely hints at the more impassioned moments of debate that produced it. Here we see page two of the original four-page document, which is displayed daily at the National Archives in Washington, D.C.

67. The framers initially limited impeachable offenses to treason and bribery. Late in the debates, George Mason moved to add "maladministration" to the list, but this seemed so vague and subjective that the framers adopted "high Crimes and Misdemeanors" instead. That phrase had a venerable history in England, dating to the fourteenth century, but the framers did not discuss how it would be translated into American practice. Even so, its addition widened a clause that originally was tightly drawn into an open-ended formula that made the collective judgment of the House of Representatives the basic criterion for determining what an impeachable offense might be.

Accusations of impeachable presidential misconduct have (thankfully) been too few and infrequent to permit a coherent doctrine of impeachment to evolve. There was ample reason to impeach Andrew Johnson for his systematic efforts to thwart the Reconstruction of the defeated Confederacy, but his trial in 1868 came too late to prevent or undo the damage he had done. In 1974 the full House of Representatives would certainly have improved the impeachment bill brought by its Judiciary Committee against Richard Nixon for his involvement in covering up the Watergate burglary, had he not resigned in disgrace first. The impeachment of Bill Clinton in 1999 for private acts unrelated to his presidential duties was arguably an act of partisan spite that placed the bar for impeachable offenses as low as it could conceivably go, but whether it set a precedent that future Congresses would follow remains to be seen.

Section 4. The President, Vice President and all civil Officers of the United States, shall be removed from Office on Impeachment for, and Conviction of, Treason, Bribery, or other high Crimes and Misdemeanors.[67]

68. In Britain, judicial power was still regarded as an aspect of executive power, and providing justice to royal subjects was one of the chief duties of the crown. Beginning with the state constitutions of 1776, Americans treated the judiciary as an independent if distinctly inferior department of government, and the existence of a separate article governing the judiciary confirms that critical shift in constitutional thinking. Yet in terms of American practice, juries, not judges, were the principal sources of legal authority, deemed competent to decide matters of law and fact alike.

The Constitution establishes the Supreme Court, but leaves it to Congress to determine how many members it will have. The framers were uncertain whether national laws should be adjudicated solely in federal courts, or could be safely enforced by state courts, whose judges were bound by the Supremacy Clause of Article VI to obey the federal Constitution and laws above the conflicting legal authority of the states.

The principle of judges serving "during good Behaviour" was first established in the parliamentary Act of Settlement of 1701, which fixed the succession to the British throne on the Electors of the German state of Hanover. Judges had previously served at the pleasure of the crown, and in the heated controversies of the seventeenth century, they often acted as the pliant agents of the Stuart monarchs. Independent tenure did not turn English judges into a separate branch or department of government, in the way in which Article III treats the federal judiciary. In adopting the British standard of "good Behaviour" (which we casually but not inaccurately call "life tenure"), the framers were also taking a significant step toward creating a professional class of qualified judges

ARTICLE III

Section 1. The judicial Power of the United States, shall be vested in one supreme Court, and in such inferior Courts as the Congress may from time to time ordain and establish. The Judges, both of the supreme and inferior Courts, shall hold their Offices during good Behaviour, and shall, at stated Times, receive for their Services, a Compensation, which shall not be diminished during their Continuance in Office.[68]

who could act as an independent source of legal authority. The adoption of the Federal Constitution thus contributed to a significant shift in the locus of legal decision making, away from juries and into the hands of judges, and it thereby promoted the professionalization of legal practice more generally.

69. These important clauses define and in critical ways limit the jurisdiction of federal courts. Their power extends only to "cases" and "controversies," meaning real disputes between identifiable parties. Federal courts cannot act in an advisory capacity to the other branches of government, or rule on the constitutionality of legislation or other actions until presented with a genuine dispute. Cases have repeatedly been contrived, however, in which spurious sets of facts have provided courts with a pretext for issuing important rulings, as in the carriage-tax case, *Hylton v. United States* (1796), which was the first occasion on which the Supreme Court upheld a contested act of Congress on constitutional grounds.

In English and American jurisprudence, "Cases in Equity" involve disputes in which the ordinary rules and remedies of common-law courts do not apply. The rules of equity are generally regarded as being more flexible than common law. Rather than simply require the payment of damages well after a wrong has been committed, for example, courts acting in equity can issue injunctive relief immediately prohibiting the offensive action from continuing. In England, the crown established a separate Court of Chancery, independent of the ordinary common-law courts of justice, to fulfill this function. The Constitution, instead, allows federal courts to exercise equitable jurisdiction as a normal power.

Section 2. The judicial Power shall extend to all Cases, in Law and Equity, arising under this Constitution, the Laws of the United States, and Treaties made, or which shall be made, under their Authority;—to all Cases affecting Ambassadors, other public Ministers and Consuls;—to all Cases of admiralty and maritime Jurisdiction;—to Controversies to which the United States shall be a Party;—to Controversies between two or more States;—between a State and Citizens of another State;—between Citizens of different States,—between Citizens of the same State claiming Lands under Grants of different States, and between a State, or the Citizens thereof, and foreign States, Citizens or Subjects.[69]

The general jurisdiction of the federal judiciary is stated in terms of two distinct categories of cases: one based on subject matter, the other on the identity of the parties. Matters relating to acts of national governance and international relations clearly belong within the federal realm, but so do cases where reliance on the courts of one state might enable provincial prejudices and preferences to shape the outcomes improperly. Given the prominent role of juries in the eighteenth century, relying on state courts to pass judgment on the claims of out-of-state litigants might have seemed a risky venture.

70. Empowering the Supreme Court to review the factual findings of lower courts, Anti-Federalists misleadingly argued, would nullify the traditional authority of trial-level juries.

71. Anti-Federalists argued that by explicitly requiring jury trial for criminal cases, this clause effectively eliminated it for civil cases. Federalists answered that because the states did not uniformly mandate jury trials for civil suits, the Constitution conformed to American practice, and Congress could always permit juries to sit on civil cases as well.

72. Treason is the sole crime that the Constitution strictly defines, proscribing the ability of the government to expand the scope of this grave offense against the state. Charges of treason were frequently leveled for political reasons during the Tudor and Stuart eras, and that experience provides the deep background against which the framers dealt with this one offense so carefully.

In all Cases affecting Ambassadors, other public Ministers and Consuls, and those in which a State shall be Party, the supreme Court shall have original Jurisdiction. In all the other Cases before mentioned, the supreme Court shall have appellate Jurisdiction, both as to Law and Fact, with such Exceptions, and under such Regulations as the Congress shall make.[70]

The Trial of all Crimes, except in Cases of Impeachment, shall be by Jury; and such Trial shall be held in the State where the said Crimes shall have been committed; but when not committed within any State, the Trial shall be at such Place or Places as the Congress may by Law have directed.[71]

Section 3. Treason against the United States, shall consist only in levying War against them, or in adhering to their Enemies, giving them Aid and Comfort. No Person shall be convicted of Treason unless on the Testimony of two Witnesses to the same overt Act, or on Confession in open Court.[72]

73. Just as John Locke argued that the rights a conqueror gains over his defeated foes on the battlefield do not extend to their families or descendants, so the Constitution limits the punishment for treason to the perpetrators alone.

74. A similar clause appeared in the Articles of Confederation, but here Congress receives additional power to enforce the legal respect that states owe one another.

The final phrase, "the Effect thereof," provides the basis on which Congress enacted a key provision of the Defense of Marriage Act (DOMA) of 1996, adopted in response to the movement to legalize the marriage of same-sex couples. The opening words of this clause have the force of a legal command, and the use of the term "Full Faith" implies that states cannot waver over which legal actions they will respect. But allowing Congress to determine "the Effect" can be read to mean that Congress can also say "no effect," which is exactly what DOMA did by absolving states of any duty to respect same-sex marriages performed elsewhere. Constitutional challenges to this act have so far failed, yet opponents of same-sex marriages would prefer to have the ambiguity resolved by a further constitutional amendment defining marriage solely as a union between a man and a woman. Numerous states have adopted corresponding acts defining marriage in just those terms. Yet public opinion on the issue remains fluid, and it is questionable whether Congress would approve such an amendment or whether the necessary three-fourths of the states would ratify it.

The Congress shall have Power to declare the Punishment of Treason, but no Attainder of Treason shall work Corruption of Blood, or Forfeiture except during the Life of the Person attainted.[73]

ARTICLE IV

Section 1. Full Faith and Credit shall be given in each State to the public Acts, Records, and judicial Proceedings of every other State. And the Congress may by general Laws prescribe the Manner in which such Acts, Records and Proceedings shall be proved, and the Effect thereof.[74]

75. An American citizen moving from one state to another, or simply conducting affairs in another state, is entitled to the same legal rights and treatment as the state's own citizens. The specific "Privileges and Immunities of Citizens," an early Supreme Court opinion held, would "be more tedious than difficult to enumerate," but they certainly embraced an array of basic civil liberties. The clause was restated in Section 1 of the Fourteenth Amendment, but to little interpretive effect.

76. Once again the Constitution uses a euphemism to avoid explicitly mentioning slavery. The original wording spoke of persons "legally held to Service or Labour." But some framers thought this endorsed "the idea that slavery was legal in a moral view." The word "legally" was accordingly deleted and a new phrase substituted. By combining this clause with the "Necessary and Proper" Clause, Congress could claim authority to enact laws regulating procedures for the return of fugitive slaves, as it did in 1793 and 1850. Left ambiguous was whether free states had to comply actively with the recovery of human property. In its 1842 decision in *Prigg v. Pennsylvania,* the Supreme Court prohibited the states from interfering with recapture, but left them under no positive obligation to assist in the enforcement of the original act of 1793. Northern states responded with personal liberty laws effectively barring their officials from aiding the recovery of fugitive slaves. In response, a strengthened Fugitive Slave Act became part of the last great intersectional negotiation, the Compromise of 1850. Bitter objections to its enforcement in the North and the passions that this opposi-

Section 2. The Citizens of each State shall be entitled to all Privileges and Immunities of Citizens in the several States.[75]

No Person held to Service or Labour in one State, under the Laws thereof, escaping into another, shall, in Consequence of any Law or Regulation therein, be discharged from such Service or Labour, but shall be delivered up on Claim of the Party to whom such Service or Labour may be due.[76]

tion engendered in the South contributed to the mounting political crisis of the 1850s.

77. This section initially operated as a mutual guarantee among the original states, acknowledging their existing jurisdictions and territorial claims and barring separatist movements from attempting to detach territory and seek legal recognition. It does not explicitly stipulate that new states are to be admitted on terms of full equality with the original states, and the convention in fact deleted language to that effect. Even so, that understanding has guided the interpretation of this section since ratification.

While the Convention of 1787 was meeting, the Continental Congress approved the landmark Northwest Ordinance of that year, providing for the admission of new states in the lands to be settled north of the Ohio River. Congress had acquired jurisdiction over this territory through the voluntary cessions of territorial claims by Virginia, New York, Massachusetts, and Connecticut. In a sense, the cessions operated as an extra-constitutional amendment to the Articles of Confederation, which did not vest the Continental Congress with the authority to acquire territory to be governed under its own jurisdiction.

A similar question arose, at least within the fertile mind of President Thomas Jefferson, over the Louisiana Purchase of 1803. Nothing in the Constitution explicitly authorized the government to increase the territory of the United States, and Jefferson was apparently troubled by the idea that the admission of so many new states as the territory could support would transform the very nature of the nation. Yet the offer made by Napoleon was too good to

Section 3. New States may be admitted by the Congress into this Union; but no new State shall be formed or erected within the Jurisdiction of any other State; nor any State be formed by the Junction of two or more States, or Parts of States, without the Consent of the Legislatures of the States concerned as well as of the Congress.[77]

refuse, and it could easily be argued that every nation possesses an inherent power to acquire territory by treaty or conquest. Jefferson went so far as to draft a constitutional amendment that would not only have legitimated the purchase, but committed the nation to using the territory acquired as a reserve for Native American peoples.

Is West Virginia constitutional? Early in the Civil War its inhabitants broke away from the seceding slave state of Virginia, which obviously would never consent to this loss of territory. It was for Congress to decide whether its application for admission to the Union as a free state was legitimate, and so Congress did in December 1862. But Lincoln was uncertain whether to sign the bill, and his cabinet was divided on the point. Finally he assented, less because he was convinced it was constitutional than in deference to expedient circumstances and in recognition that a precedent set amid the confusion of the Civil War would have little if any value at other times.

78. In the Missouri Crisis of 1819–1821, those who wished to bar the further migration of slaves into Missouri as a condition of statehood treated "all needful Rules and Regulations" as roughly synonymous with the "Necessary and Proper" formula of Article I. Those who wished to see Missouri become a slave state argued that such "Rules and Regulations" applied only to territorial matters narrowly defined and to federal property. Some years later, the Mormon advocates of polygamy in the Utah Territory argued, unsuccessfully, that Congress could not use its legislative authority

The Congress shall have Power to dispose of and make all needful Rules and Regulations respecting the Territory or other Property belonging to the United States; and nothing in this Constitution shall be so construed as to Prejudice any Claims of the United States, or of any particular State.[78]

under this clause to prohibit their adherence to "the Principle" of plural marriage.

79. Because the Constitution does not explain what a "republican form of government" is, it is difficult to say how this guarantee would be applied, beyond prohibiting the states from creating a monarchy or a hereditary aristocracy. The immediate source of this clause was Shays's Rebellion of 1787, which the Continental Congress was powerless to suppress. The clause also empowered the national government to assist in putting down slave rebellions. It was invoked in the litigation arising from the Dorr Rebellion of 1842, an episode in which two rival governments vied for control of that tiny piece of real estate known as Rhode Island. One government was elected under the state's old royal charter, which largely restricted suffrage to rural freeholders; the other represented an insurgent democratic movement based on universal manhood suffrage. In *Luther v. Borden,* a cautious Supreme Court held that the dispute was nonjusticiable (not a matter for legal resolution) and that application of the Guarantee Clause to this situation required a political determination by Congress. After the Civil War, some thought was given to invoking the clause as a basis for the Reconstruction of the South, but Congress turned instead to the newly proposed Fourteenth Amendment.

Section 4. The United States shall guarantee to every State in this Union a Republican Form of Government, and shall protect each of them against Invasion; and on Application of the Legislature, or of the Executive (when the Legislature cannot be convened) against domestic Violence.[79]

ARTICLE V

The Congress, whenever two thirds of both Houses shall deem it necessary, shall propose Amendments to this Constitution, or, on the Application of the Legislatures of two thirds of the several States, shall call a Convention for proposing Amendments, which, in either Case, shall be valid to all Intents and Purposes, as Part of this Constitution, when ratified by the Legislatures of three fourths of the several States, or by Conventions in three fourths thereof, as the one or the other Mode of Ratification may be proposed by the Congress; Provided that no Amendment which may be made prior to the Year One thousand eight hundred and eight shall in any Manner affect the first and fourth

80. Requiring amendments to be approved by supermajorities in both houses of Congress and the states creates a virtually insuperable barrier to serious constitutional revision. But by abandoning the unanimity rule of the Confederation, and proposing two separate routes by which changes could be either proposed or ratified, the framers thought they were lowering the obstacles to amendment. Had comparable procedures been in effect in the 1780s, the amendments to the Confederation proposed by the Continental Congress would have been adopted, obviating the need for anything like the Convention of 1787.

The first proviso restricting the use of the amending power was inserted at the behest of the South Carolina and Georgia delegations, in the expectation that their constituents would wish to renew the active importation of African slaves to make up for losses incurred during the wartime occupation of those states by the British. As soon as the prescribed interval passed, Congress barred the further importation of slaves.

The final proviso makes the equal state vote in the Senate the sole clause of the Constitution that Article V cannot reach. It thus ensures that the American practice of political representation at the national level of government will never be consistent with the fundamental democratic principle of one person, one vote.

81. One main purpose of the Federalist movement of the late 1780s was to establish the public credit of the United States. By committing the new government to assume the Revolutionary War debt of the Confederation, this provision laid the foundation for the ambitious financial program that Treasury Secretary Hamilton pre-

Clauses in the Ninth Section of the first Article; and that no State, without its Consent, shall be deprived of its equal Suffrage in the Senate.[80]

ARTICLE VI

All Debts contracted and Engagements entered into, before the Adoption of this Constitution, shall be as valid against the United States under this Constitution, as under the Confederation.[81]

sented to Congress in 1790. Preserving and honoring the Revolutionary debt would help make the case for levying the taxes and raising the revenue needed to make the new federal government a viable enterprise. It would also give the public creditors a powerful incentive to devote their political loyalties to the Union.

82. The Supremacy Clause first appeared in the New Jersey Plan of June 1787 as a weak alternative to the proposal of the Virginia Plan giving Congress a veto over state laws. Initially the clause made no mention of the authority of the state constitutions. But with little debate or controversy, the framers gradually expanded the clause into its more sweeping form. The final provision effectively assumed that state judges would exercise a power of judicial review, at least when federal constitutional questions came before them, even though that doctrine was not yet generally or wholly accepted within the states as part of their individual constitutional orders.

83. Religious tests for officeholding or voting were common in both the American states and Britain. The Massachusetts constitution of 1780, for example, required officials to declare that they "believe the Christian religion, and have a firm persuasion of its truth." Questions about the personal religious convictions of the framers and other leading members of their generation continue to trouble Americans today. Were they devout Christians or rational deists who could contentedly attend religious services yet remain skeptical about the divinity of Jesus, the truth of revelation, and the plausibility of any of a number of biblical miracles? Many, like Madison, kept their religious beliefs to themselves, but this

This Constitution, and the Laws of the United States which shall be made in Pursuance thereof; and all Treaties made, or which shall be made, under the Authority of the United States, shall be the supreme Law of the Land; and the Judges in every State shall be bound thereby, any Thing in the Constitution or Laws of any State to the Contrary notwithstanding.[82]

The Senators and Representatives before mentioned, and the Members of the several State Legislatures, and all executive and judicial Officers, both of the United States and of the several States, shall be bound by Oath or Affirmation, to support this Constitution; but no religious Test shall ever be required as a Qualification to any Office or public Trust under the United States.[83]

provision offers a powerful testament to the idea that such convictions were deemed irrelevant to holding public office.

84. This formula violated the Confederation in two ways. It allowed the Constitution to take effect without the unanimous approval of all thirteen states, and it allowed that approval to be expressed not by the state *legislatures* but by elected conventions that would embody the sovereignty of the people in a purer, more direct form. In the ensuing ratification campaign, Federalists insisted that the conventions had to accept or reject the Constitution in its entirety, not approve or reject it in its separate parts. Once nine states ratified, the nonconsenting states would be under greater pressure to come in as well. This proved a decisive factor in the key state of New York, where opponents of the Constitution held a decided majority at the time of the convention.

85. Referring to the "Unanimous Consent of the States present" enabled the signers to pass silently over the fact that three delegates declined to sign (or even "witness") the completed Constitution: George Mason and Edmund Randolph of Virginia, and Elbridge Gerry of Massachusetts.

ARTICLE VII

The ratification of the Conventions of nine States, shall be sufficient for the Establishment of this Constitution between the States so ratifying the Same.[84]

Done in Convention by the Unanimous Consent of the States present the Seventeenth Day of September in the Year of our Lord one thousand seven hundred and Eighty-seven and of the Independence of the United States of America the Twelfth. In witness whereof we have hereunto subscribed our Names.[85]

	Geo: Read
	Gunning Bedford jun
Delaware	John Dickinson
	Richard Bassett
	Jaco: Broom
	James McHenry
Maryland	Dan of St Thos. Jenifer
	Danl. Carroll
Virginia	John Blair
	James Madison Jr.
	Wm. Blount
North Carolina	Richd. Dobbs Spaight
	Hu Williamson
	J. Rutledge
	Charles Cotesworth Pinckney
South Carolina	Charles Pinckney
	Pierce Butler
Georgia	William Few
	Abr Baldwin

G. Washington

Presidt and deputy from Virginia

New Hampshire	John Langdon Nicholas Gilman
Massachusetts	Nathaniel Gorham Rufus King
Connecticut	Wm. Saml. Johnson Roger Sherman
New York	Alexander Hamilton
New Jersey	Wil: Livingston David Brearley Wm. Paterson Jona: Dayton
Pennsylvania	B Franklin Thomas Mifflin Robt. Morris Geo. Clymer Thos. FitzSimons Jared Ingersoll James Wilson Gouv Morris

Amendments

to the

Constitution

In transmitting its proposed amendments to the states, the First Congress evidently felt it had to explain why the Constitution was being revised so soon after it went into operation. The problem was not that the Constitution as adopted was really defective, Congress implied. Prompt adoption of the amendments would help "prevent misconstruction or abuse of its powers" and enhance "public confidence." Nothing of substance was being altered; rather, the meaning of the Constitution was somehow being enhanced and clarified.

When James Madison introduced his proposed amendments in the House of Representatives on June 8, 1789, he wanted them to be individually inserted, or interwoven, in the text of the Constitution at those points where each seemed most salient. But Roger Sherman, the former framer from Connecticut, repeatedly protested that Congress had no authority to alter the text of the Constitution as it came from the Federal Convention, and his view ultimately prevailed. Amendments, if approved, would appear as supplemental articles. In his introductory speech, Madison casually described his amendments as a "bill of rights," and that is the name by which, over time, Americans have come to know the first ten supplemental articles to the Constitution. Just *how well* they know what their rights are becomes, periodically, a matter of civic or educational concern. Public opinion polls repeatedly indicate that alarming portions of the citizenry have only the haziest notion of the content of the Bill of Rights. From the vantage point of 1788, this would be disturbing indeed. For when Anti-Federalists argued that a Constitution lacking a bill of rights was flawed, they imagined that such documents would work best not as legal texts

Congress of the United States

Begun and held at the City of New-York, on
Wednesday the fourth of March, one thousand
seven hundred and eighty nine.

THE Conventions of a number of the States,
having at the time of their adopting the Constitution,
expressed a desire, in order to prevent misconstruction
or abuse of its powers, that further declaratory and re-
strictive clauses should be added: And as extending the
ground of public confidence in the Government, will
best ensure the beneficent ends of its institution.

RESOLVED by the Senate and House of
Representatives of the United States of America, in

to be cited or pled in court but as educational statements reminding the people of the fundamental principles of republican government.

1. As drafted and ratified, the protection for these fundamental rights of freedom of thought and expression applied only against the national government, not the states. But over time, and with the authority of the Fourteenth Amendment, the "no law" formula came to stand for the more radical principle that there are realms of individual belief and behavior that no government should be allowed to regulate. If Congress cannot restrict these rights, why should any other government be allowed to do so?

The First Congress tried different ways of expressing the basic relation between state and church. Madison's original language was: "nor shall any national religion be established." The House proposed "no law establishing religion"; the Senate adopted a narrower formula, prohibiting "establishing articles of faith or a mode of worship." The conference committee proposed the final, open-ended language, but without further definition. By the Revolutionary era, many states supported multiple establishments—meaning they provided public aid for an array of Protestant denominations. Because this amendment, like the rest of the Bill of Rights, originally operated only as a restraint upon Congress, its main purpose was to ensure that the regulation of all those state-based establishments would be free from the threat of federal interference. Today this Establishment Clause is generally equated with the principle of separation of church and state, but originally it was simply

Congress assembled, two thirds of both Houses concurring, that the following Articles be proposed to the
Legislatures of the several States, as amendments to
the Constitution of the United States, all, or any of
which Articles, when ratified by three fourths of the
said Legislatures, to be valid to all intents and purposes,
as part of the said Constitution; viz.

ARTICLES in addition to, and Amendment of the
Constitution of the United States of America, proposed by Congress, and ratified by the Legislatures of
the several States, pursuant to the fifth Article of the
original Constitution.

AMENDMENT I (1791)

Congress shall make no law respecting an establishment of religion, or prohibiting the free exercise
thereof; or abridging the freedom of speech, or of the
press; or the right of the people peaceably to assemble,
and to petition the government for a redress of grievances.[1]

a matter of federalism. States could establish religion in any of a number of ways; Congress could not do so at all.

"Free exercise" is also a broader term than "freedom of conscience." The latter implies a right to *believe* whatever one wishes in matters of faith and salvation, but the former suggests a right to *practice* one's religion openly, without restraint. Yet in an admittedly confused, complicated, and hotly contested realm of jurisprudence, American courts have often equated exercise with belief, a distinction that may reflect the deeply Protestant origins of the dominant American religious culture, with its emphasis on faith over works or liturgy. The initial leading case, *Reynolds v. United States* (1878), effectively held that the Mormon practice of polygamy could not be legally justified on free-exercise grounds. Modern free-exercise doctrine has been skeptical of allowing individuals to claim religious exemptions from laws of general applicability. Yet it has also recognized a need to ascertain whether the government has a compelling interest in regulating the practice in question.

Historically, freedom of speech was a right of legislators, to be secured against the crown, but by 1776 Americans were treating it as a right of citizens against government in general.

In Anglo-American law, freedom of the press originally meant that government could not *prevent* the publication of works it deemed offensive, but printers and authors were still legally liable for printing seditious libels demeaning the authority of government or the character of officials. One could be punished for libel even if the accusation made could be proved true. Under the Sedition Act of 1798, a Federalist Congress seemingly ignored the plain

Anti-Federalists proposed scores of amendments to the Constitution. But when James Madison set out to allay their concerns, he carefully limited his proposed alterations almost exclusively to the protection of rights, rejecting the structural changes Anti-Federalists really desired. Seen here is the first page of the twelve amendments Congress sent to the states in 1789.

text of this clause, but it did so under the prior legal understanding that freedom of the press meant only no prior restraint. In a doctrinal sense, the Sedition Act marked a step forward in legal thinking by allowing the truth of an accusation to be argued as a defense.

The right to petition long represented one of the essential ways in which individuals related to the state, though as supplicants more than as citizens. But the language of this clause seems to treat the right as a collective one, to be exercised by a significant segment of the community expressing its political will. Anti-Federalists would have extended this right to allow communities to issue instructions to their elected members of the House of Representatives, just as state legislators were sometimes instructed by their constituents.

2. The amendment originated in Anti-Federalist concerns that Congress might misuse its power of "organizing, arming, and disciplining the Militia" to neglect it entirely. The militia might be disarmed, George Mason warned the Virginia ratification convention, not by federal confiscation of private firearms, but simply by Congress's failure to keep militiamen adequately equipped (or "well regulated," in eighteenth-century usage). That neglect, in turn, would make it easier for the "standing army" Congress would control to trample the reserved rights of citizens and states.

In recent decades, the National Rifle Association and its supporters have waged a vigorous campaign to argue that the amendment was really meant to protect a personal right to keep arms for purposes of individual self-defense, and that the preamble to this

AMENDMENT II (1791)

A well regulated militia, being necessary to the security of a free state, the right of the people to keep and bear arms, shall not be infringed.[2]

clause did not limit its purpose to the militia alone. Though the historical evidence for that view is tenuous, in 2008 the Supreme Court sustained the individual-rights reading in its decision in *District of Columbia v. Heller,* overturning a broad prohibition on the private ownership of handguns in the nation's capital. The Court reached this conclusion by largely ignoring the actual debates that led to the adoption of the amendment. Corresponding provisions in numerous state constitutions now assert an individual right to own and use firearms in language much more explicit than the much-disputed formula of 1789.

3. This amendment seems to protect only a narrowly defined right against a very specific practice—and one that can still be suspended in wartime. In 1765 and 1774, Parliament passed Quartering Acts authorizing the housing of British soldiers in privately owned American buildings. But these acts were merely extensions of the Mutiny Acts that Parliament had enacted *annually* since 1689, a procedure that reflected a deep conviction that the entire administration of military matters should be subject to strict legislative authority.

The practice of quartering soldiers in private homes was one of the tactics used by the French state to harass Huguenots (French Protestants) into renouncing their faith during the persecutions accompanying the revocation of the Edict of Nantes in 1685. Their sufferings figured prominently in the new ideas of human rights that began to form at the close of the seventeenth century.

AMENDMENT III (1791)

No soldier shall, in time of peace be quartered in any house, without the consent of the owner, nor in time of war, but in a manner to be prescribed by law.[3]

4. The dual requirements that searches and seizures (or arrests) be reasonable, not arbitrary or capricious, and that the warrants authorizing them be based upon "probable cause," not vague suspicion or idle curiosity, represent a reaction against the British practice of general warrants, which gave officials an open-ended, discretionary power to conduct searches. The use of a form of general warrant called a "writ of assistance" in *Paxton's Case* (tried in Boston in 1761) made this issue a *cause célèbre* in the colonies.

"Unreasonable" and "probable" are themselves inherently ambiguous terms, and modern Fourth Amendment jurisprudence presents courts with endless interpretive challenges, covering everything from the right of drunk drivers to refuse sobriety tests to the use of various forms of electronic surveillance, including the mass monitoring of telephone conversations and email correspondence through the techniques of data mining. In the landmark case of *Mapp v. Ohio* (1961), the Supreme Court held that evidence improperly obtained could be excluded from trial, giving police departments across the country a strong incentive to develop scrupulous procedures for the acquisition and safeguarding of evidence. Six years later, in *Katz v. United States,* the Court overturned a gambling conviction based on the unauthorized use of a recording device placed outside a phone booth. The purpose of the Fourth Amendment, the Court held, was to protect an individual's reasonable expectation of privacy, and not merely to guard certain obvious places (one's home or office) from the physical intrusion of surveillance. But the question of whether innocent or unintentional error in conducting searches and seizures should be excluded remains a subject of controversy.

AMENDMENT IV (1791)

The right of the people to be secure in their persons, houses, papers, and effects, against unreasonable searches and seizures, shall not be violated, and no warrants shall issue, but upon probable cause, supported by oath or affirmation, and particularly describing the place to be searched, and the persons or things to be seized.[4]

5. The Fifth Amendment contains one of the Constitution's most familiar provisions, well known to the American public for being invoked in congressional hearings by witnesses declining to answer potentially incriminating questions and for the repetition of the so-called Miranda warning in countless television dramas ("You have the right to remain silent; anything you say may be used in court against you"). The amendment as a whole combines three fundamental common-law rights relating to criminal prosecutions (formal accusation by a grand jury, and the protections against double jeopardy and self-incrimination) with an expansive statement of the idea of "due process of law" and protection for the basic right of property. A traditional reading of "due process of law" merely requires that defendants and litigants be properly served with the correct writs for the legal proceedings in which they are involved. But by echoing the basic trinity of the natural rights to life, liberty, and property, Madison converted this narrow legal requirement into a broader affirmation that government actions affecting the rights of individuals must conform to established standards of legality.

The final clause (known as the Takings Clause) reflected Madison's fear that popularly elected legislatures would show little respect for basic rights of property—or rather, that they would favor the economic interests of the many over the vested rights and larger holdings of the few. Possibly this clause was also a response to the wartime purchase of crops and other supplies needed by the Continental Army with financial instruments that the Continental Congress and the states were ill-equipped to redeem fairly. In the important case of *Barron v. Baltimore* (1833), a unanimous Supreme

ANNOTATIONS

AMENDMENT V (1791)

No person shall be held to answer for a capital, or otherwise infamous crime, unless on a presentment or indictment of a grand jury, except in cases arising in the land or naval forces, or in the militia, when in actual service in time of war or public danger; nor shall any person be subject for the same offense to be twice put in jeopardy of life or limb; nor shall be compelled in any criminal case to be a witness against himself, nor be deprived of life, liberty, or property, without due process of law; nor shall private property be taken for public use, without just compensation.[5]

Court held that the Takings Clause, and other clauses of the Bill of Rights, applied only against the federal government, not against the states. That reading was true to the original understanding of 1789–1791, but it would eventually be overturned when the Court began using the Fourteenth Amendment to "incorporate" most provisions of the Bill of Rights against the states.

"Presentment" occurs when the citizen members of a grand jury, rather than government officials, initiate prosecutions. It harks back to the traditional practice of entrusting essential aspects of law enforcement not to the government but to informed and responsible members of the community.

6. The Constitution originally required only that jury trials be held in the state where the crime had occurred. Anti-Federalists argued that the government could willfully abuse this power to drag defendants far from their homes and from the scene of their crime, increasing the cost and difficulty of mounting an adequate defense.

As originally understood, the final clause granting the right to legal counsel merely preserved a defendant's option to employ a lawyer in his defense; it did not require the state to provide counsel for him. The modern reinterpretation of this clause to require the provision of effective legal counsel to indigent defendants in any criminal proceeding is often regarded as one of the great heroic stories of American jurisprudence. It began with the Supreme Court's decision in *Powell v. Alabama* (1932), the famous "Scottsboro Boys" case in which nine young African Americans were falsely accused of raping two white women, given a speedy trial of

AMENDMENT VI (1791)

In all criminal prosecutions, the accused shall enjoy the right to a speedy and public trial, by an impartial jury of the state and district wherein the crime shall have been committed, which district shall have been previously ascertained by law, and to be informed of the nature and cause of the accusation; to be confronted with the witnesses against him; to have compulsory process for obtaining witnesses in his favor, and to have the assistance of counsel for his defence.[6]

the kangaroo-court variety, convicted, and sentenced to death. The defendants were provided with legal representation, but it could charitably be described as incompetent. The Supreme Court overturned their conviction, not because the defendants lacked counsel specifically under the Sixth Amendment, but because the totality of circumstances violated the Due Process Clause of the Fourteenth Amendment. Yet it is at least conceivable that, with effective legal representation, the Scottsboro Boys could have challenged their trial and the evidence against them far more readily.

Six years later, in *Johnson v. Zerbst,* the justices held that the right to counsel was an essential requirement for federal criminal trials, and that courts should closely scrutinize the circumstances under which a defendant was said to waive that right. In a subsequent decision, however, the Court retreated from the implication that the *states* could be routinely required to provide counsel for indigents, largely because of the enormous expense this would impose. Finally, in the landmark case of *Gideon v. Wainwright* (1963), the Warren Court overturned this precedent in one of the major decisions signaling the onset of its "revolution" in criminal justice—a revolution that would affect state-based procedures more profoundly than their federal counterparts. Subsequent decisions tested and defined exactly when the right to counsel is triggered. In *Escobedo v. Illinois* (1964), the Court treated the refusal of police to honor a suspect's repeated requests to be allowed to consult his lawyer as a constitutionally impermissible denial of the Sixth Amendment right to counsel. But in subsequent cases, notably *Miranda v. Arizona,* the justices placed greater emphasis on the Fifth Amendment right against self-incrimination, so that early access to counsel be-

The widely publicized Alabama trial of the nine "Scottsboro Boys," falsely accused of raping two white women while riding a freight train, was a prelude to the Supreme Court's eventual expansion of the Sixth Amendment right to counsel in criminal trials. The defendants, seen in this 1931 photo, were legally (but also incompetently) represented at the excessively speedy trial where they were convicted and sentenced to death. When the Supreme Court overturned their conviction in 1932, it did so because the totality of circumstances in their trial violated the Due Process Clause of the Fourteenth Amendment. Yet the case also raised important questions about what the effective right to counsel meant—questions that the Court pursued in later rulings.

came instrumentally important for supporting a suspect's right to remain silent.

7. To the modern eye, the twenty-dollar minimum seems to represent a great anachronism. The qualifying phrase "at common law" excludes suits arising under either equity or admiralty law, and arguably does not cover matters governed by statute. The real purpose of the Seventh Amendment, however, was not to identify a monetary value per se, but to answer two other Anti-Federalist charges against the Constitution. The first was that its failure to require jury trials for civil cases was tantamount to their abolition or prohibition, under the legal principle *expressio unius, exclusio alterius* (that is, the positive expression of one thing and the omission of another implies the exclusion of the latter). The second charge was that the Supreme Court's appellate jurisdiction over matters of fact as well as law could allow the justices to overturn the factual findings of juries, and thus negate the high value that the common law placed on the judgment of ordinary jurors representing the community, rather than on that of appointed judges.

8. The language exactly tracks Article 9 of the Virginia Declaration of Rights of 1776—except that Madison substituted the verb "shall" for "ought," implying that the Constitution was stating a binding command rather than a general principle. But the crux of these three provisions lies in their adjectives. The modifiers "excessive" and "cruel and unusual" illustrate what legal scholars call the differences between *rules* and *standards*. A *rule* flatly states a requirement that authorities must follow; a *standard* implies the exis-

AMENDMENT VII (1791)

In suits at common law, where the value in controversy shall exceed twenty dollars, the right of trial by jury shall be preserved, and no fact tried by a jury, shall be otherwise reexamined in any court of the United States, than according to the rules of the common law.[7]

AMENDMENT VIII (1791)

Excessive bail shall not be required, nor excessive fines imposed, nor cruel and unusual punishments inflicted.[8]

tence of a discretionary range of possible actions that can vary according to the circumstances of the defendant or the sentiments of an entire era. Words like these cry out for interpretation—and perhaps nowhere more so than in defining what is "cruel and unusual," a phrase that has been a major point of contention in the ongoing debate over the morality of capital punishment and the various ways in which it is executed upon the condemned.

9. No body of jurisprudence has ever given content to this amendment, and it lies inertly in the Constitution, a joker that has never been played. Yet its origins go to the heart of the public debate that ultimately produced the Bill of Rights, and indeed to the key shift in the very understanding of the authority of constitutional documents that took place in the decade after 1776. Prior to independence, the American colonists traced the origins of the rights they claimed to multiple sources: God or nature, customs or common law, even a birthright inherited from the pioneering activities of the first settlers. Rights did not derive their authority from the bare fact of being mentioned in a legal or constitutional text; rather, the fact that they were mentioned merely confirmed their existence. After 1776, however, Americans came to regard written constitutions as supreme, fundamental law; and in that case, the best way to identify and secure rights would be to entrench them in a constitutional text. But if that was where rights now derived their full legal power, it followed that the omission of a right, or the failure to state it adequately, might weaken or compromise—or "deny and disparage"—its authority. A right omitted from the Con-

AMENDMENT IX (1791)

The enumeration in the Constitution, of certain rights, shall not be construed to deny or disparage others retained by the people.[9]

stitution but recognized only in statute, or at common law, would be relegated to an inferior status.

The Ninth Amendment attempts to solve that problem by asserting that omission need not be construed as relegation. But it fails to explain exactly how an unenumerated right can become a fundamental one, and that is why the amendment has been only a constitutional teaser. Could it, for example, provide a plausible foundation on which to ground a woman's right to abortion, or the broader if more nebulous concept of a right to privacy, recognized in the 1965 case *Griswold v. Connecticut?* In a concurring opinion, Justice Arthur Goldberg implied that the Ninth Amendment might work better than the majority's reference to "penumbras formed by emanations" from other clauses of the Bill of Rights, but he did not speak for the majority, and the thought still lies there, tempting but inert.

10. This formula is commonly described as a "truism" that does not alter or amend the Constitution in any way. Powers not delegated are not delegated; powers not prohibited to the states are not prohibited; and if any powers are left over, they belong either to the people or the states. This amendment was conceived as a way to reassure Anti-Federalists who feared that the Necessary and Proper Clause and the Supremacy Clause would enable the national government to run roughshod over the states. But it seems doubtful that they really were placated, because Anti-Federalist congressmen in 1789 thought this language would have little value unless it was altered to read "powers not expressly delegated."

Still, if regarded simply as a principle, the Tenth Amendment

AMENDMENT X (1791)

The powers not delegated to the United States by the Constitution, nor prohibited by it to the states, are reserved to the states respectively, or to the people.[10]

has had a greater impact than the Ninth. It has often provided a rallying point for states'-rights proponents, beginning with Thomas Jefferson and many of his acolytes in the early nineteenth-century Republican Party, and again for opponents of expansive national power in more recent times. Some modern commentators argue, too, that one of the reserved natural rights of the people is the right to "alter or abolish governments" recognized in the early state constitutions, a right that might be exercised outside the Article V amendment procedures of the Constitution.

11. The first amendment directly framed to overturn a decision of the Supreme Court was a reaction to the Supreme Court's decision in *Chisholm v. Georgia* (1793), supporting the right of the plaintiff, a resident of South Carolina, to seek restitution, as the executor of an estate, for debts contracted during the Revolutionary War. Article III brought suits between a state and citizens of another state within the purview of federal courts, but also placed suits to which a state was a party under the original jurisdiction of the Supreme Court. Georgia, in the first of many instances in which it would raise the banner of state sovereignty, declined to appear when the Court heard Chisholm's plea, tacitly relying on the common-law doctrine of sovereign immunity, which holds that a sovereign government cannot be sued without its consent. The justices heard the case and ruled 4-to-1 for Chisholm. As was the custom, each justice wrote his own opinion, and their opinions directly confronted one of the great questions of American constitutional theory: Where did sovereignty reside in the new federal republic, and did the states retain enough of it to invoke some residual concep-

AMENDMENT XI (1795)

The Judicial power of the United States shall not be construed to extend to any suit in law or equity, commenced or prosecuted against one of the United States by Citizens of another State, or by Citizens or Subjects of any Foreign State.[11]

tion of sovereign immunity in their favor? James Wilson, one of the concurring justices, had astutely addressed this general question during the constitutional debates of 1787–1788, arguing that the entire conception of sovereignty that Americans inherited from Europe was irrelevant to their case. Sovereignty, the ultimate authority in a polity, was not vested in any institution or level of government, he had argued. It belonged to the people, who could parcel out such parts of it as they wished to nation and states alike. It followed that a Constitution adopted with the consent of the American people could modify or even abrogate a doctrine of sovereign immunity that was ultimately rooted in the idea that the crown could be petitioned by its loyal subjects but not sued. Unfortunately for the majority in *Chisholm,* Americans—or at least their elected representatives—greeted this decision with a firestorm of protest, and this amendment was quickly framed and ratified as a result.

Much more recently, the Eleventh Amendment became a source of some controversy when a sharply divided Supreme Court issued a series of rulings expanding the scope of sovereign immunity well beyond the specific wording of the constitutional text. The decisions in these cases may be read less as a careful legal analysis of an admittedly complex doctrine than a reflection of the desire of the Rehnquist Court's conservative majority to restore some notion of the inherent sovereignty of the states as a corrective to the expansion of federal legislative power since the New Deal. Writing for the Court in *Alden v. Maine* (1999), Justice Anthony Kennedy observed that the "dignity" of the states was insulted by federal statutes authorizing a state's own citizens to sue the state in its own

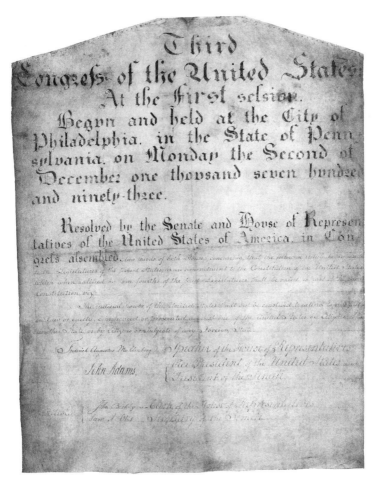

The Eleventh Amendment was a direct response to the Supreme Court's ruling in *Chisholm v. Georgia*, permitting an out-of-state creditor to sue an ostensibly sovereign state without its consent. The signature of Vice President John Adams appears on this official text of the amendment in his capacity as president of the Senate, a duty that Adams took very seriously.

courts. One could as easily argue that the dignity of a republican state is affirmed, not diminished, when the actions of its governing agencies, themselves the creatures of a sovereign people, are liable to legal challenge.

AMENDMENT XII (1804)

The electors shall meet in their respective states and vote by ballot for President and Vice President, one of whom, at least, shall not be an inhabitant of the same state with themselves; they shall name in their ballots the person voted for as President, and in distinct ballots the person voted for as Vice President, and they shall make distinct lists of all persons voted for as President, and of all persons voted for as Vice President, and of the number of votes for each, which lists they shall sign and certify, and transmit sealed to the seat of the government of the United States, directed to the President of the Senate;—The President of the Senate shall, in the presence of the Senate and House of Representatives, open all the certificates and the votes shall then be counted;— the person having the greatest number of votes for President, shall be the President, if such number be a majority of the whole number of electors appointed; and if no person have such majority, then from the persons having the highest numbers

In the presidential election of 1800, the two Republican running mates, Thomas Jefferson and Aaron Burr (depicted here in a stipple engraving by Enoch G. Gridley, after a portrait by John Vanderlyn) each received seventy-three electoral votes, throwing the election into the outgoing House of Representatives, which was controlled by Federalists. The Twelfth Amendment prevented this glitch from recurring by requiring electors to cast separate designated ballots for president and vice president.

not exceeding three on the list of those voted for as President, the House of Representatives shall choose immediately, by ballot, the President. But in choosing the President, the votes shall be taken by states, the representation from each state having one vote; a quorum for this purpose shall consist of a member or members from two thirds of the states, and a majority of all the states shall be necessary to a choice. And if the House of Representatives shall not choose a President whenever the right of choice shall devolve upon them, before the fourth day of March next following, then the Vice President shall act as President, as in the case of the death or other constitutional disability of the President. The person having the greatest number of votes as Vice President, shall be the Vice President, if such number be a majority of the whole number of electors appointed, and if no person have a majority, then from the two highest numbers on the list, the Senate shall choose the Vice President; a quorum for the purpose shall consist of two thirds of the whole

12. In the presidential election of 1800, Republican candidates Thomas Jefferson and Aaron Burr each received seventy-three electoral votes, a majority of all the votes cast. But Article II instructed each elector to cast two votes for president, not separate votes for president and vice president, and the Republicans failed to take the steps necessary to throw a few votes away from Burr. Jefferson was the obvious head of his Republican Party, Burr only a key ally. The electoral tie between them sent the final selection into the lame-duck House of Representatives, where the defeated Federalists would cast the decisive votes. Federalist leaders were profoundly suspicious of Jefferson on principle. But the *éminence grise* of their party, Alexander Hamilton, detested Burr, his New York City rival and the man who eventually took Hamilton's life in their famous duel at Weehawken. After a week was spent on thirty-six indecisive ballots, the abstentions of several Federalist congressmen switched Maryland and Vermont to Jefferson, while Delaware and South Carolina were recorded as abstaining.

The amendment made two significant changes in Article II: it required electors to vote separately for president and vice president, and it reduced from five to three the number of candidates from whom the House would choose if no contender received a majority of electoral votes. The amendment could, and perhaps should, have done more. As first proposed by the House, it would also have required the division of states into electoral districts, and thus denied state legislatures the option of deciding how electors were to be appointed. The Senate, mindful of protecting the authority of its own constituents, the same legislatures, demurred.

An even more radical step would have been to reconsider the

number of Senators, and a majority of the whole number shall be necessary to a choice. But no person constitutionally ineligible to the office of President shall be eligible to that of Vice President of the United States.[12]

idea of a national popular election. The two contests of 1796 and 1800 had demonstrated what the framers had doubted: that the political system could give an informed people an effective choice between two leading candidates. But the allocation of electoral votes by states worked to the advantage of the South, because of the Three-Fifths Clause. The longevity of the Virginia dynasty (Washington, Jefferson, Madison, and Monroe) brought increasing denunciations of the electoral system in the North, to no constitutional avail.

13. Three-score years had passed since the previous successful amendment. A conviction had taken hold that the original Constitution was the sacred legacy of the founding generation, something not to be trifled with unless—as in the previous two amendments—some specific provision needed urgent correction. Adoption of the Thirteenth Amendment signaled not only the onset of Reconstruction but a new attitude about the Constitution and the Union it embodied.

The amendment also solved the surprisingly difficult question of how to complete the great project of abolishing "slavery"—a word now making its first and only appearance in the Constitution. The Emancipation Proclamation applied only to slaves behind southern lines, and the three amendments that Lincoln had proposed to Congress in pursuit of emancipation were gradualist measures that would give the nonseceding border states where slavery was still legal (Maryland, Delaware, Kentucky, and Missouri) incentives for abolition and would compensate masters who remained loyal to the Union for their lost property. The longer the

AMENDMENT XIII (1865)

Section 1. Neither slavery nor involuntary servitude, except as a punishment for crime whereof the party shall have been duly convicted, shall exist within the United States, or any place subject to their jurisdiction.

Section 2. Congress shall have power to enforce this article by appropriate legislation.[13]

war ground on, with its horrific toll in lives lost, the more emancipation seemed its only just end, particularly when slaves revealed their own longing and capacity for freedom by seeking refuge behind Union lines and enlisting as soldiers themselves. Even then, Congress was slow to think of a constitutional amendment as the best means to achieve emancipation with one decisive stroke. It took an unlikely coalition of northern Democrats, eager to take the slavery question out of politics entirely, and abolitionists to push the amendment alternative forward.

Many previous amendments had contained multiple clauses, but this was the first to be divided into two numbered sections. Section 1 appears to be what lawyers call a "self-executing" provision: it issues a command that is legally sufficient in itself. Yet Section 2 supposes that further legal action may be necessary, and gives Congress explicit authority to determine what that action may be. The designation of Congress as the institution to act by *legislation* implies a distrust of the will and capacity of the Supreme Court, an institution still tainted by the memory of the *Dred Scott* case (1857), to respond judicially to the opposition that emancipation might spark.

This last photograph of the Great Emancipator was taken on April 9, 1865, five days before his assassination by John Wilkes Booth. The hollow cheeks, sunken eyes, and distracted expression capture the physical and psychological toll four years of Civil War had exacted on Lincoln. Three weeks earlier, Lincoln had given his magnificent Second Inaugural Address, a deeply religious text echoing the famous passage in *Notes on the State of Virginia* in which Thomas Jefferson trembled for his nation as he contemplated the severe decree that a just God would impose on Americans for the evil of slavery.

14. None of the constitutional provisions adopted since 1789 has done more to shape and define the concept of "a more perfect Union" than Section 1. None comes closer to Madison's 1787 vision of a national government capable of correcting injustices originating within the states

In drafting Section 1, the congressional Joint Committee on Reconstruction had two main objectives. One was to repudiate and reverse Chief Justice Taney's holding in *Dred Scott* that African Americans (even when free!) could never enjoy the status of citizens; they were, in his blatantly racist language, "so far inferior, that they had no rights which the white man was bound to respect." By simple birthright, the freed slaves could now claim and exercise the two distinct sets of rights that all Americans possessed as citizens both of the nation and the state of their residence, and they would do so on the foundation of legal equality. The second objective of Section 1 was to provide constitutional authority for the legislative power that Congress, in the Civil Rights Act of 1866, was already exercising on behalf of the freedmen. The unreconstructed governments of the South, many still dominated by the old ruling class, had imposed so-called Black Codes designed to keep former slaves in a state of peonage by denying such fundamental civil rights as the right to own property, sue or testify in court, and freely contract for their labor. These were all traditional subjects of state law, but also realms of behavior the Civil Rights Act sought to reach.

Given the ambitious purposes the Fourteenth Amendment was meant to serve, the Privileges and Immunities, Due-Process, and Equal-Protection clauses were designed to reinforce one another

AMENDMENT XIV (1868)

Section 1. All persons born or naturalized in the United States, and subject to the jurisdiction thereof, are citizens of the United States and the State wherein they reside. No State shall make or enforce any law which shall abridge the privileges or immunities of citizens of the United States; nor shall any State deprive any person of life, liberty, or property, without due process of law; nor deny to any person within its jurisdiction the equal protection of the laws.[14]

as they provided a three-pronged basis for assuring the civil and constitutional rights of the freedmen. The key feature of these three provisions is that they make the acts of all state and local authorities subject to federal review. The framers of the amendment may have expected the Privileges and Immunities Clause to do the heaviest work by identifying a body of rights that state and local governments would thereafter have to respect. Those privileges and immunities would probably include the fundamental rights enumerated in the first eight amendments to the Constitution. Many of the amendment's leading framers and supporters believed that the Supreme Court had erred in holding that the Bill of Rights did not apply to the states. But the history of the interpretation of Section 1 tells a different story. Inevitably, the broad remedies it promised became the subject of massive amounts of litigation, starting with the *Slaughterhouse* case of 1873. Over time, the Supreme Court narrowly interpreted Privileges and Immunities to cover only a miscellaneous set of rights that derived specifically from national citizenship.

The burden of fulfilling the amendment's promise instead fell on the final two provisions of Section 1. The Due Process Clause has its own tangled history, bound up with the Court's invention of the concept of "substantive due process." Read narrowly, due process means only that government acts should conform to recognized legal procedures. But when the Court reclothed due process in substantive dress, it gave a new array of meanings to the two key words "liberty" and "property." Some aspects of liberty and property were so fundamental that they could be insulated against any effective government regulation, even when the actions affected

In 1846, Dred Scott (pictured here in a daguerreotype by J. H. Fitzgibbon, circa 1858), born into slavery, sued for his freedom, arguing that his previous residence in the free state of Illinois and the free territory of Minnesota released him from slavery and made him a citizen of the United States. A U.S. Supreme Court decision on March 6, 1857, held that African Americans—even if free—had never been regarded as citizens and could never attain that status. By granting citizenship to "all persons born or naturalized in the United States," the opening sentence of the Fourteenth Amendment (ratified in 1868) reversed the Supreme Court's ruling in *Dred Scott.*

were not explicitly recognized as constitutional rights. Notions of substantive due process undergird two of the most controversial judicial decisions in American constitutional history: *Lochner v. New York* (1905), overturning a statute regulating the working hours of bakers as a violation of a fundamental freedom to contract one's labor, and *Roe v. Wade* (1973), establishing a constitutional right to abortion.

Lochner gave its name to an era of jurisprudence in which the Supreme Court was often vilified for restricting progressive regulatory legislation in the name of respect for the elusive economic rights of substantive due process. From a modern perspective, the corresponding villain in the history of the Equal Protection Clause was the Court's 1896 decision in *Plessy v. Ferguson,* legitimating the practices of racial segregation and discrimination that flourished in southern states after the end of Reconstruction in 1877. *Plessy* upheld a Louisiana law permitting railways to provide "separate but equal" accommodations for the different races. The lone dissenter was John Marshall Harlan, and his simple ringing statement that "our constitution is color-blind, and neither knows nor tolerates classes among citizens," remains one of the most celebrated pronouncements in U.S. history. Unlike *Lochner,* the decision in *Plessy* was neither controversial nor even remarkable at the time it was handed down. Three-score years later, the Court repudiated the *Plessy* doctrine in *Brown v. Board of Education,* the epochal decision that launched the larger project of disassembling the legal edifice of racial segregation and discrimination.

After Reconstruction, white-dominated governments in the South began to create a new legal regime of racial discrimination and segregation. In its 1896 decision in *Plessy v. Ferguson*, a case involving segregated rail cars in Louisiana, the Supreme Court gave its approval to these practices under what came to be known as the "separate but equal" doctrine. Racial separation became a rule of life in much of the South, as embodied in segregated schools, hotels, restaurants, even bathrooms and drinking fountains, duly marked with signs designating "colored" and "white" facilities. This 1939 photograph shows a drinking fountain for "colored" patrons in an Oklahoma City streetcar terminal.

15. Taken alone, the first sentence seems superfluous. Simple ratification of the Thirteenth Amendment eliminated the category "other persons" that served as a euphemism for slaves in the Three-Fifths Clause. Indeed, one irony of emancipation was that the southern share of seats in the House of Representatives would increase because African Americans would now count as full persons for purposes of apportionment. That increase would occur regardless of whether ex-slaves voted, because apportionment was tied solely to population. In framing this section, Congress discussed tying representation to voter turnout, not mere population. But because only males could vote, that would produce a disparate impact between long-settled eastern states and newer western states, where migration factors tilted the gender ratio in favor of males. The alternative was to penalize southern states if they ever restricted African American voting. But enforcement depended on the willpower of Congress; and when whites regained control of southern governments after 1877, and actively began stripping freedmen of the right to vote they had vigorously exercised, Congress defaulted on its duty.

Section 2. Representatives shall be apportioned among the several States according to their respective numbers, counting the whole number of persons in each State, excluding Indians not taxed. But when the right to vote at any election for the choice of electors for President and Vice President of the United States, Representatives in Congress, the Executive and Judicial officers of a State, or the members of the Legislature thereof, is denied to any of the male inhabitants of such State, being twenty-one years of age, and citizens of the United States, or in any way abridged, except for participation in rebellion, or other crime, the basis of representation therein shall be reduced in the proportion which the number of such male citizens shall bear to the whole number of male citizens twenty-one years of age in such State.[15]

16. To the dismay and anger of northern Republicans, the southern delegations that journeyed to Washington in the fall of 1865, naively expecting to take their seats in the Thirty-Ninth Congress, were filled with former Confederate officials and officers. The generosity with which President Andrew Johnson, successor to the martyred Lincoln, was dispensing pardons to former Confederates also troubled Republicans. A bloody and destructive Civil War had not been waged, they believed, to allow the old ruling class of the South to return to national power. Section 3 would prevent this. An earlier version adopted by the House of Representatives would have prohibited those who had willingly supported the Confederacy from voting in federal elections before 1870.

Section 3. No person shall be a Senator or Representative in Congress, or elector of President and Vice President, or hold any office, civil or military, under the United States, or under any state, who, having previously taken an oath, as a member of Congress, or as an officer of the United States, or as a member of any state legislature, or as an executive or judicial officer of any state, to support the Constitution of the United States, shall have engaged in insurrection or rebellion against the same, or given aid or comfort to the enemies thereof. But Congress may by a vote of two thirds of each House, remove such disability.[16]

17. It can hardly be surprising that a public debt incurred in support of a failed insurrection would have to be repudiated. What might strike a modern reader as more puzzling is the idea that a master might claim compensation for the "loss or emancipation of any slave"—that is, a person whose lifetime labor had been wholly expropriated to the benefit of another. But prior to 1861, slaves were recognized and treated as the legal property of their owners, and protection of the rights of property had long been a fundamental value of Anglo-American legal thinking. One of the recurring arguments against earlier emancipationist schemes involved asking who would pay the costs of compensating masters for the loss of their economic rights to slave labor.

18. Earlier drafts of the Fourteenth Amendment placed this provision in Section 1 and explicitly echoed the "Necessary and Proper" wording of Article I, Section 8.

Section 5 has become a subject of controversy since the Supreme Court's decision in *City of Boerne v. Flores* (1997), overturning the federal Religious Freedom Restoration Act. In that decision, the Court held that the Section 5 power to *enforce* rights does not give Congress the authority to define the substantive scope of those rights. Speaking in the imperious voice so typical of its modern jurisprudence, the Court held that it alone could make decisions as to the substance and content of constitutional rights. Such a brash statement would have confounded the authors of Section 5, who came to their task convinced that the same institution that had decided *Dred Scott* less than a decade earlier might not always be the sole or wisest guardian of rights.

ANNOTATIONS

Section 4. The validity of the public debt of the United States, authorized by law, including debts incurred for payment of pensions and bounties for services in suppressing insurrection or rebellion, shall not be questioned. But neither the United States nor any state shall assume or pay any debt or obligation incurred in aid of insurrection or rebellion against the United States, or any claim for the loss or emancipation of any slave; but all such debts, obligations and claims shall be held illegal and void.[17]

Section 5. The Congress shall have power to enforce, by appropriate legislation, the provisions of this article.[18]

19. When Reconstruction began, the Republicans of the Thirty-Ninth Congress were divided over whether to grant freedmen the right to vote. Some believed that access to suffrage would provide former slaves with the greatest security they could enjoy, but others doubted whether a people emerging from two centuries of bondage were ready to exercise the most treasured right of all. Nor did public opinion in the North support African American suffrage. In the Reconstruction Act of 1867, Congress enfranchised male African American voters in the South, and Republicans relied on their votes to gain and maintain control of state governments in the former Confederacy. As Democrats recovered political strength in the North, and as whites resorted to violence to suppress the black vote in the South, congressional Republicans overcame their reluctance to entrench the freedmen's right to vote in the Constitution. Yet even then the amendment did not grant a positive or absolute right to vote, but was instead framed as a prohibition against the use of "race, color, or previous condition of servitude" to deny suffrage. This left open a path to find surrogate legal means of preventing African Americans from voting. Following the end of Reconstruction in 1877, southern Democrats began using expedients such as literacy tests and poll taxes to suppress the African American vote. At first these measures met opposition from poor whites, who would also be adversely affected; but by the close of the century the campaign for legal disfranchisement, supported by violence and an indifferent North, was achieving its goal. The promise of the amendment was not fully realized until the Voting Rights Act of 1965 helped to launch the Second Reconstruction.

AMENDMENT XV (1870)

Section 1. The right of citizens of the United States to vote shall not be denied or abridged by the United States or by any state on account of race, color, or previous condition of servitude.

Section 2. The Congress shall have power to enforce this article by appropriate legislation.[19]

Though we often like to think that the history of the right to vote is a story of steady expansion in pursuit of democratic ideals, opposition to enlarging the electorate has been a recurring motif in American political history. Anti-immigrant and particularly anti-Catholic sentiment supported efforts to restrict access to suffrage in the nineteenth century, and the disfranchisement of felons has been criticized as an effective way to limit voting by minority groups that have high rates of incarceration.

20. Every American's favorite amendment, because it places citizens in annual direct contact with their government, also marked a renewed expression of the idea that the Constitution was a document that could actually be amended. The amendment was a delayed corrective to the Supreme Court's widely lambasted decision in *Pollock v. Farmers' Loan and Trust* (1895), which reversed a number of precedents narrowly defining the direct taxes requiring apportionment among the states on the basis of population. The vastly expanded revenues the income tax provided have enabled the federal government, through its spending power, to become the dominant force of social policy.

AMENDMENT XVI (1913)

The Congress shall have power to lay and collect taxes on incomes, from whatever source derived, without apportionment among the several States, and without regard to any census or enumeration.[20]

21. The popular election of senators became one of the great reform causes of the late nineteenth century, fueled by the perception that the Senate was a club for the wealthy and that seats there were often gained through improper collusion and corruption. The insurgent Populist Party endorsed popular election in 1892, and Democrats followed suit in 1900. In the years 1893–1902, the House of Representatives approved forerunners of the eventual amendment by the requisite supermajorities six times. When the Senate killed all these proposals in committee, however, the locus of political action shifted to the states. By 1912, thirty-one state legislatures had indicated their support for the change, revealing that they no longer wished to retain the privilege the Constitution granted them.

Increasing numbers of states also instituted various kinds of primary elections to identify the candidates voters favored, and legislators felt bound to honor those results. A key innovation came from Oregon, which in 1904 began requiring candidates for the legislature to indicate whether they would support the election of whichever candidate carried the state primary, regardless of party. The success of the Oregon method led to its imitation elsewhere. The federal senators elected under these changing procedures had no reason to honor the traditional practice. When Congress again considered the amendment in February 1911, it fell four votes short of the two-thirds supermajority in the Senate. There was significant turnover in the new Senate that convened the next month, and in June a revised version passed easily. But the two houses disagreed over another issue: whether the amendment should include language parallel to Article I, Section 4, which empowers Congress

AMENDMENT XVII (1913)

The Senate of the United States shall be composed of two Senators from each State, elected by the people thereof, for six years; and each Senator shall have one vote. The electors in each State shall have the qualifications requisite for electors of the most numerous branch of the State legislatures.

When vacancies happen in the representation of any State in the Senate, the executive authority of each State shall issue writs of election to fill such vacancies: Provided that the legislature of any State may empower the executive thereof to make temporary appointments until the people fill the vacancies by election as the legislature may direct.

This amendment shall not be so construed as to affect the election or term of any Senator chosen before it becomes valid as part of the Constitution.[21]

to supersede state electoral practices. By invoking that principle, Congress might have been perceived as threatening the South's successful efforts to disfranchise and suppress African American voters. The final language conceded that point to the South.

The popular election of the Senate has obviously made the modern Congress as a whole a more democratic institution than the one the framers of the Constitution bequeathed to posterity. But it also illustrates continuing deficiencies and ambiguities in the American practice of constitutional democracy. Unlike the districts of the House of Representatives, states cannot be gerrymandered for partisan ends. Senatorial elections are free from the sophisticated manipulation of political geography that accompanies the decennial reapportionment of House seats. On the other hand, there is a sense in which the states, those building blocks of federalism, are themselves inherently gerrymandered entities—artificial lines on a vast map that inevitably produce significant population disparities among the jurisdictions they establish.

In this famous photograph from 1921, New York City deputy police commissioner John A. Leach supervises the disposal of beer into the sewer, following a raid during Prohibition. Under increasing pressure from the temperance movement, the Senate proposed the Eighteenth Amendment on December 18, 1917. Ratified on January 16, 1919, it prohibited "the manufacture, sale, or transportation of intoxicating liquors."

22. Prohibition can be described as the only successful effort, however brief, to convert a social policy into a constitutional mandate. For the temperance movement, it marked a dramatic culmination of decades of efforts to reverse the prodigious increase in alcohol consumption that followed the Revolution, turning the nation into what one historian has called an "alcoholic republic" where much of the population spent its days in semi-inebriation, tippling as they worked. Reformers enjoyed significant success in many states, and especially in rural areas where the pulse of old-time religiosity and moral crusades beat most fiercely. They were far less successful in urban areas where immigrants fresh from the Old World congregated. The temperance campaign, it must be said, also betrayed a deep anti-Catholic animus.

No other amendment, before or since, has empowered the states to use their own concurrent initiative to administer a federal policy. The amendment was also the first to adopt a sunset provision for ratification. It was initially conceived by Warren G. Harding, the future lackluster president, in the hope that the deadline would pass and the amendment would die without the necessary votes being attained. But the amendment proved surprisingly popular and ratification came speedily. So, in the ordinarily glacial pace of constitutional time, did repeal.

AMENDMENT XVIII (1919)

Section 1. After one year from the ratification of this article the manufacture, sale, or transportation of intoxicating liquors within, the importation thereof into, or the exportation thereof from the United States and all territory subject to the jurisdiction thereof for beverage purposes is hereby prohibited.

Section 2. The Congress and the several States shall have concurrent power to enforce this article by appropriate legislation.

Section 3. This article shall be inoperative unless it shall have been ratified as an amendment to the Constitution by the legislatures of the several States, as provided in the Constitution, within seven years from the date of the submission hereof to the States by the Congress.[22]

23. Supporters of women's rights were bitterly disappointed when the Forty-First Congress, drafting the Fifteenth Amendment, excluded sex from the protected categories that could no longer be used to deny African Americans the right to vote. Antislavery and temperance were the two great public causes that had drawn women into public life since the 1820s, and their labors there should have proved that they were fully qualified to deliberate on public matters—that they were at least as qualified to do so as the ex-slaves of the South.

With the constitutional option closed, suffragists focused their efforts on the states, and women's right to vote made slow if steady progress. When they did gain the right to vote, the heavens did not tremble, the earth did not stand still, existing political alignments remained intact—and arguments that there was something to fear in female suffrage lost credibility.

No additional amendment was required to make women eligible for election or appointment to federal office. The first woman to serve in Congress, Representative Jeanette Rankin of Montana, was elected in 1917, prior to the adoption of the amendment. Until the adoption of the Fifteenth Amendment, the language of the Constitution had been gender neutral, with the exception of the use of the male pronoun to refer to the president in Article II. The greater barriers to full participation in political life that women encountered after 1919 thus owed more to entrenched social and cultural attitudes than to formal legal prohibitions.

AMENDMENT XIX (1920)

The right of the citizens of the United States to vote shall not be denied or abridged by the United States or by any State on account of sex.

Congress shall have power to enforce this article by appropriate legislation.[23]

American women had been actively seeking the right to vote since the mid-nineteenth century. Many were sorely disappointed when the language of the Fourteenth and Fifteenth amendments endorsed the notion that only men could properly exercise the suffrage. Here suffragists picket outside the White House in 1917. The concisely worded Nineteenth Amendment, ratified on August 18, 1920, guaranteed that the right to vote "shall not be denied or abridged by the United States or by any State on account of sex."

AMENDMENT XX (1933)

Section 1. The terms of the President and Vice President shall end at noon on the 20th day of January, and the terms of Senators and Representatives at noon on the 3d day of January, of the years in which such terms would have ended if this article had not been ratified; and the terms of their successors shall then begin.

Section 2. The Congress shall assemble at least once in every year, and such meeting shall begin at noon on the 3d day of January, unless they shall by law appoint a different day.

Section 3. If, at the time fixed for the beginning of the term of the President, the President elect shall have died, the Vice President elect shall become President. If a President shall not have been chosen before the time fixed for the beginning of his term, or if the President elect shall have failed to qualify, then the Vice President elect shall act as President until a President

24. This amendment brought national government into the modern era by ending the normal thirteen-month interval between the election of a new Congress and its first meeting. It also advanced the inauguration of the president by six weeks. The amendment was sent to the states in March 1932 and unanimously ratified within thirteen months. Their enthusiasm can be explained by the fact that consideration of the amendment coincided with the depths of the Great Depression, amid a pained awareness that the discredited administration of Herbert Hoover would remain in office for four months after his foreordained defeat to Franklin Roosevelt, and that the Congress charged with devising a fresh plan of recovery could not meet until March.

Some contemporary critics of the Constitution still find the interval between the election and inauguration of a new administration unconscionable. After all, parliamentary democracies with strong political party systems and "shadow governments" can transfer power within a few days; the United States still requires more than two months, and it is the rare presidential candidate who begins serious planning for the staffing of an administration before his election.

shall have qualified; and the Congress may by law provide for the case wherein neither a President elect nor a Vice President elect shall have qualified, declaring who shall then act as President, or the manner in which one who is to act shall be selected, and such person shall act accordingly until a President or Vice President shall have qualified.

Section 4. The Congress may by law provide for the case of the death of any of the persons from whom the House of Representatives may choose a President whenever the right of choice shall have devolved upon them, and for the case of the death of any of the persons from whom the Senate may choose a Vice President whenever the right of choice shall have devolved upon them.

Section 5. Sections 1 and 2 shall take effect on the 15th day of October following the ratification of this article.[24]

25. The proponents of repealing the failed experiment of Prohibition understood that temperance forces might well be able to stall or block ratification by bringing pressure to bear on state legislatures. Accordingly, this is the only amendment to follow the alternative path of ratification, being submitted to popularly elected conventions in the states.

Section 2 left the states in full possession of their traditional police powers over the sale and consumption of liquor. Several states used this authority to limit or bar the interstate shipment of wine directly to consumers, not for reasons of public welfare, but essentially as a protectionist measure to favor their own in-state producers. In the age of e-commerce, this policy seemed arbitrary, and in 2005 the Supreme Court ruled that states could not bar interstate shipments directly to consumers while allowing intrastate shipments to go unregulated.

AMENDMENT XXI (1933)

Section 1. The eighteenth article of amendment to the Constitution of the United States is hereby repealed.

Section 2. The transportation or importation into any State, Territory, or possession of the United States for delivery or use therein of intoxicating liquors, in violation of the laws thereof, is hereby prohibited.

Section 3. This article shall be inoperative unless it shall have been ratified as an amendment to the Constitution by conventions in the several States, as provided in the Constitution, within seven years from the date of the submission hereof to the States by the Congress.[25]

Prohibition became increasingly unpopular during the Great Depression, especially in large urban centers, where European immigrants wondered why Americans were so averse to the enjoyment of one of life's great pleasures. Here, at an anti-Prohibition parade and demonstration in Newark, N.J., on October 28, 1932, protesters carry placards reading, "We Want Beer." On December 5, 1933, the ratification of the Twenty-First Amendment repealed Prohibition (the Eighteenth Amendment).

Franklin Delano Roosevelt was president from 1933 to 1945, having been elected to four terms in office. He is the only president to have served more than two terms. Roosevelt is seen here delivering his fourth inaugural address, on January 20, 1945, outside the south portico of the White House. Many photographs of FDR were carefully staged to avoid any hint of the disabling bout of polio he suffered in August 1921. Shortly after his final inauguration, he embarked on the physically taxing trip to the Yalta Conference with Stalin and Churchill that likely hastened his death on April 12, 1945. The Twenty-Second Amendment, ratified on February 27, 1951, set a two-term limit for the presidency.

26. The two-term precedent set by George Washington proved impossible to break, and prior to 1940 only two of the other nine men who served two terms seemed to desire a third (Ulysses Grant and Theodore Roosevelt, who was promoted to the presidency by McKinley's assassination near the beginning of his second term and who ran again as the Bull Moose third-party candidate in 1912). But in 1940, with war raging in Europe and Asia, Franklin Roosevelt threw tradition aside and won reelection, as he did again in 1944. When the Republicans briefly regained control of Congress in 1947, they quickly pushed this amendment through, with support from southern Democrats who had grown disillusioned with FDR. There was little evidence of public support for the two-term limit, however, and after securing strongly partisan approval in Republican-dominated legislatures (except for Massachusetts) in 1947, the amendment seemed to founder. Its eventual ratification in 1951 depended significantly on support from southern states, all dominated by Democrats, who appear to have embraced the Republican position in reaction to the pro–civil rights position of their national party. Once it was ratified, some Republicans began to express misgivings when they realized that their own popular president, Dwight Eisenhower, could easily have won a third term (though he clearly preferred to go golfing).

Like other term-limit ideas, this one has an antidemocratic character to it, denying the people the right to reelect an incumbent they like. Yet one wonders whether the demands of the modern presidency are more than any individual can reasonably be expected to bear for more than the eight years the Constitution allows. Presidents seem to age visibly before our eyes — not as badly,

AMENDMENT XXII (1951)

Section 1. No person shall be elected to the office of the President more than twice, and no person who has held the office of President, or acted as President, for more than two years of a term to which some other person was elected President shall be elected to the office of the President more than once. But this Article shall not apply to any person holding the office of President when this Article was proposed by Congress, and shall not prevent any person who may be holding the office of President, or acting as President, during the term within which this Article becomes operative from holding the office of President or acting as President during the remainder of such term.

Section 2. This Article shall be inoperative unless it shall have been ratified as an amendment to the Constitution by the legislatures of three fourths of the several States within seven years from the date of its submission to the States by the Congress.[26]

perhaps, as Franklin Roosevelt appeared to have done in the famous photos taken during his last months of life, yet still in noticeable ways.

27. As originally approved by the Senate, this amendment would have granted residents of the District of Columbia representation in the House, as well as a right to appoint electors for presidential elections. Fortunately for tourists who loved visiting Washington to see the nation's funniest license plates ("TAXATION WITHOUT REPRESENTATION"), the House pared the amendment down to its current form. There is a plausible constitutional objection against granting the District a voting member in the House, for Article I declares that the House "shall be composed of Members chosen . . . by the People of the several States," and Washington is a city, not a state. Yet that literalist reading of the text also violates a deeper norm of republican government. For the founding generation, the guiding principle of popular representation was that a legislative assembly should be a "mirror" or "portrait" of the larger society. Yet residents of the District of Columbia never get to see their reflection or sit for the painter. A simpler explanation of why the District is denied representation is that its demography ensures that the member so chosen would be a Democrat, and Republicans oppose extending the right on that basis.

AMENDMENT XXIII (1961)

Section 1. The District constituting the seat of Government of the United States shall appoint in such manner as the Congress may direct:

A number of electors of President and Vice President equal to the whole number of Senators and Representatives in Congress to which the District would be entitled if it were a State, but in no event more than the least populous State; they shall be in addition to those appointed by the States, but they shall be considered, for the purposes of the election of President and Vice President, to be electors appointed by a State; and they shall meet in the District and perform such duties as provided by the twelfth article of amendment.

Section 2. The Congress shall have power to enforce this article by appropriate legislation.[27]

28. By 1960 the poll tax was an almost moribund vestige of the great suppression of the African American vote in the South that began in the late nineteenth century. Only five states retained it, but with sit-ins and freedom rides pushing civil rights to the forefront of American politics in the early 1960s, its abolition became an important symbol of the nation's changing attitudes toward race. In framing the amendment to cover primary as well as general elections, however, Congress paid indirect homage to one of the Supreme Court's pioneering decisions in the realm of civil rights. In *Smith v. Allwright* (1944), the Court had overturned a Texas Democratic Party rule prohibiting blacks from voting in primary elections, which, in the old one-party South, was where the outcomes of most elections were usually determined. The state, the Court ruled, was sufficiently enmeshed in the legal conduct of primaries to be subject to damages under the Fifteenth Amendment.

Because this amendment applied only to federal elections, several southern states attempted to maintain the poll tax for separately held state elections, but the Supreme Court overturned that practice in *Harper v. Virginia Board of Elections* (1966) as a violation of the Equal Protection Clause of the Fourteenth Amendment.

AMENDMENT XXIV (1964)

Section 1. The right of citizens of the United States to vote in any primary or other election for President or Vice President, for electors for President or Vice President, or for Senator or Representative in Congress, shall not be denied or abridged by the United States or any State by reason of failure to pay any poll tax or other tax.

Section 2. The Congress shall have power to enforce this article by appropriate legislation.[28]

29. An immediate context for the Twenty-Fifth Amendment was the assassination of President John F. Kennedy on November 22, 1963. The nature of his wounds raised the possibility that a president might survive in office while being gravely impaired. But the amendment also addresses a larger cluster of issues relating to presidential succession.

Article II says only that the duties of the presidency shall "devolve" on the vice president in these cases (and in the case of disability). Starting with the first case of presidential succession in 1841 (John Tyler), all vice presidents succeeding to the office had acted as presidents and been regarded as such. This provision simply removes any ambiguity as to the successor's status.

30. Both of Madison's vice presidents, George Clinton and Elbridge Gerry, died in office. Five others followed their example, and the office was left vacant nine other times—eight times by presidential succession, and once by John C. Calhoun's resignation. Congress can (and has) set the further line of succession by statute, but the ever-increasing importance of the presidency justifies giving as much political credibility to a successor as possible. Even if a congressional appointment is a weak substitute for a vote of the people, it does give Congress an opportunity to examine the president's nominee.

AMENDMENT XXV (1967)

Section 1. In case of the removal of the President from office or of his death or resignation, the Vice President shall become President.[29]

Section 2. Whenever there is a vacancy in the office of the Vice President, the President shall nominate a Vice President who shall take office upon confirmation by a majority vote of both Houses of Congress.[30]

Section 3. Whenever the President transmits to the President pro tempore of the Senate and the Speaker of the House of Representatives his written declaration that he is unable to discharge the powers and duties of his office, and until he transmits to them a written declaration to the contrary, such powers and duties shall be discharged by the Vice President as Acting President.

This photograph of President John F. Kennedy and his wife, Jackie, accompanied by Texas Governor John Connally and his wife, Nellie, was snapped moments before Lee Harvey Oswald opened fire from the Texas Book Depository in Dallas, on November 22, 1963. Kennedy suffered a fatal head wound, but the assassination raised questions about the procedures to be used to assess the status and fitness to govern of a surviving president whose health and judgment had been gravely impaired. The Twenty-Fifth Amendment was designed to amplify the inadequate rules governing presidential succession and disability laid down in the Constitution.

Section 4. Whenever the Vice President and a majority of either the principal officers of the executive departments or of such other body as Congress may by law provide, transmit to the President pro tempore of the Senate and the Speaker of the House of Representatives their written declaration that the President is unable to discharge the powers and duties of his office, the Vice President shall immediately assume the powers and duties of the office as Acting President.

Thereafter, when the President transmits to the President pro tempore of the Senate and the Speaker of the House of Representatives his written declaration that no inability exists, he shall resume the powers and duties of his office unless the Vice President and a majority of either the principal officers of the executive department or of such other body as Congress may by law provide, transmit within four days to the President pro tempore of the Senate and the Speaker of the House of Representatives their written declaration that the President is unable to discharge the powers and duties of his office. Thereupon Congress shall decide the is-

31. The remaining sections of the Twenty-Fifth Amendment address the problem of presidential disability, and envision two distinct scenarios. One involves a president rationally anticipating a period when he will be unable to perform his duties, notably while undergoing planned surgery. The other assumes that the disability will happen to the president by trauma, or through a deterioration of mental faculties observable to others but not to the officeholder. The fatal wounding of President James Garfield and the massive stroke that disabled Woodrow Wilson for the final year and a half of his presidency are the most dramatic examples of this possibility, but so was the assassination attempt on President Ronald Reagan in 1981, well after the amendment was ratified. That led to a confused scene in which Secretary of State Alexander Haig went on television to assert, "I am in control here, in the White House, pending return of the vice president [George H. W. Bush]." It was not clear at the time, nor perhaps since, whether Haig was wrongly appealing to the amendment and/or the Presidential Succession Act (which places the secretary of state, as the first cabinet position established in 1789, *after* the speaker of the House and president *pro tempore* of the Senate), or simply trying to reassure the public that a responsible official was answering the phone in the Oval Office.

What gave this amendment its urgency is less the absolute indispensability of the president to the conduct of all government than the grim specter that haunted the nation at the height of the Cold War, when images of waves of nuclear-armed missiles reaching their destinations within minutes of launch required thinking of the president as an official who was potentially on duty every sue, assembling within forty-eight hours for that purpose if not in session. If the Congress, within twenty-one days after receipt of the latter written declaration, or, if Congress is not in session, within twenty-one days after Congress is required to assemble, determines by two thirds vote of both Houses that the President is unable to discharge the powers and duties of his office, the Vice President shall continue to discharge the same as Acting President; otherwise, the President shall resume the powers and duties of his office.[31]

minute of the day. That image is best captured in photographs of the military aides who carry the "nuclear football," the black suitcase packed with the necessary launch codes that accompanies the president everywhere.

Critics of the amendment find two major flaws in its mechanism for assessing presidential disability. First, it fails to require any independent or even professional medical evaluation of the president's health as a precondition for action. Second, it entrusts the decision to report a disability to subordinate officials who are themselves dependent on the president, and whose judgment might be affected by political calculations.

The Twenty-Sixth Amendment lowered the voting age in all elections to eighteen. Congress felt increasing pressure to pass the amendment as a response to the war in Vietnam, a conflict in which many American combat soldiers were draftees not yet old enough to vote. Here, on May 3, 1967, U.S. Marines carry an injured soldier to an evacuation helicopter during heavy fighting at a site known as Hill 811.

32. This amendment was badly needed for two reasons. As a general response to the political turmoil sparked by the Vietnam War, it seemed a compelling way of honoring sacrifices and burdens borne by the younger generation, who did so much of the fighting in a difficult and indecisive struggle that proved enormously controversial at home. The link between military service and suffrage ran well back into American history—to the Revolution, in fact—and this was only the most recent recognition that it was fundamentally wrong to deny the vote to those who were asked, indeed required, to risk their lives for the nation.

Congress had previously tried to achieve that end with a 1970 statute lowering the age of voting in all elections (federal, state, and local) to eighteen. Oregon challenged that law, and a splintered Supreme Court sided with the state, ruling that Congress could lower the age only for federal elections. Even this ruling rested on a rather elastic reading of the "Time, Place, and Manner" Clause of Article I, while ignoring the basic provision equating the electorate for the House of Representatives with the electorate for the lower houses of the state legislatures. States that wanted to maintain a higher voting age for their own elections would thus have to administer two ballots at the same election, a cumbersome procedure that officials naturally wanted to avoid. A constitutional amendment would resolve all that, while still paying the political debt that the Vietnam War and its bitter politics had contracted.

AMENDMENT XXVI (1971)

Section 1. The right of citizens of the United States, who are 18 years of age or older, to vote, shall not be denied or abridged by the United States or any state on account of age.

Section 2. The Congress shall have the power to enforce this article by appropriate legislation.[32]

33. The written Constitution now ends, not with a bang, or even a whimper, but with a bad joke. Originally this proposal was one of the amendments that James Madison introduced on June 8, 1789. It subsequently went to the states as the second of the twelve articles Congress submitted for their consideration in September, but was not ratified. At some point after 1791 it presumably passed from constitutional limbo to the dustbin of history—until a Texas college student named Gregory Watson read about it in a class on American government, wrote a paper on the subject, and then, as a legislative aide in Austin, launched a one-man letter-writing campaign to get the amendment ratified. Skillfully targeting the first states to act, Watson turned a quixotic quest into a constitutional bandwagon.

Though the amendment by now merely duplicated existing legislation, few causes better unite the populist mood that sometimes surges through the American body politic than resentment of Congress. Thirty-four states had ratified by 1989, three more signed on in the next two years, and then four more states put the amendment over the top in 1992. Congress could hardly say no to a movement that enjoyed so much support, and both houses adopted resolutions endorsing the idea that the amendment had been properly ratified. There is no extravagant ritual or ceremony to mark the adoption of an amendment—no parades down Pennsylvania Avenue, or fireworks on the Mall. Instead, that minor dignitary known as the Archivist of the United States certifies its ratification, as evidenced by the adopting resolutions of the states.

"No harm, no foul" may be the right philosophy for the great American game of basketball—but is it appropriate for our Con-

AMENDMENT XXVII (1992)

No law, varying the compensation for the services of the Senators and Representatives, shall take effect, until an election of Representatives shall have intervened.[33]

stitution? Perhaps in this case it is. The amendment is innocuous and inconsequential, it did enjoy a groundswell of popular support, and Congress was perfectly happy to issue its good seal of approval. Still, serious constitutionalists remain horrified by the idea that an amendment can slumber in constitutional limbo for two centuries, then be revived on a collegiate whim. Somewhere, James Madison cannot be wholly pleased, even if this proposal was originally his own.

A CALENDAR OF EVENTS

FURTHER READING

CREDITS

ACKNOWLEDGMENTS

A Calendar of Events

1607   Establishment of Jamestown, the first permanent English settlement in North America.

1619   Inaugural meeting of the Virginia House of Burgesses, the first colonial representative assembly.

1641   General Court of Massachusetts adopts the Body of Liberties of the Massachusetts Colonie in New England, an early declaration of rights.

1642   Outbreak of the English Civil War.

1649   Execution of King Charles I and abolition of the monarchy and the House of Lords. The radical Leveller movement proposes a written constitution known as the Agreement of the People.

1651   Thomas Hobbes publishes *Leviathan*.

1660   Restoration of King Charles II.

1680–1684   John Locke begins drafting his *Two Treatises of Government*,
                in the aftermath of unsuccessful efforts by three succes-
                sive Parliaments to exclude James II from succession to
                the throne.

1689   After King James II flees to France, a Convention Parlia-
                ment offers the monarchy to his daughter Mary and her
                husband, William of Orange, on condition that they ac-
                cept a Declaration of Rights recognizing the legal su-
                premacy of Parliament. Locke publishes his *Two Treatises*,
                the original Latin version of his *Letter Concerning Tolera-
                tion*, and his *Essay Concerning Human Understanding*.

1760   King George III ascends to the British throne.

1763   The Treaty of Paris confirms the British conquest of Can-
                ada. Officials in London begin considering reform of the
                imperial administration.

1765   Parliament adopts the Stamp Act taxing American colo-
                nists. Americans protest, arguing they can be taxed only
                by their own representative assemblies.

1766	Colonial protests lead to repeal of the Stamp Act, but Parliament also adopts the Declaratory Act affirming its power to legislate for the colonies "in all cases whatsoever."
1767	In a renewed effort to raise American revenues, Parliament imposes the Townshend Duties on imports of paint, paper, lead, and tea, sparking fresh colonial protests.
1770	Parliament repeals the Townshend Duties, leaving the tax on tea in place as an assertion of its authority. Despite outrage over the Boston Massacre, the colonial protest movement dissolves.
1772–1773	Political fighting between Thomas Hutchinson, the royal governor of Massachusetts, and his opponents in the colonial legislature revives the dispute over Parliament's authority in America.
1773	Parliament adopts the Tea Act, giving the bankrupt East India Company a monopoly over the sale of dutied tea in America. Colonial protests lead most tea ships to return home. But in Boston, Hutchinson's refusal to allow tea ships to sail leads to the Boston Tea Party (December 16).

1774   Parliament adopts a series of punitive measures against Massachusetts, closing the port of Boston, altering the provincial charter of government, and permitting British soldiers and officials accused of offenses against colonists to be tried in England. The First Continental Congress meets in Philadelphia (September 5–October 26) and adopts a common strategy for resisting the British measures.

1775   War begins outside Boston in April, followed by the Battle of Bunker Hill in June. The Second Continental Congress meets in May and establishes a Continental Army, commanded by George Washington. King George III declares the American colonies to be in rebellion. Parliament adopts the Prohibitory Act, subjecting colonial shipping to confiscation.

1776   In January, Thomas Paine publishes his pro-independence pamphlet *Common Sense.* Adam Smith publishes *The Wealth of Nations;* and Edward Gibbon, *The Decline and Fall of the Roman Empire.* With permission from Congress, individual colonies begin writing new constitutions of government. In April, John Adams publishes *Thoughts on Government,* outlining the basic structure of a republican constitution. Community meetings adopt resolutions calling for independence. In June, acting on resolutions approved by the provincial convention of Virginia, Congress appoints committees to frame a declaration of independence, articles of confederation, and a plan for foreign treaties. Thomas Jefferson chairs the first of these committees and takes responsibility for preparing a draft declaration. On July 2, Congress adopts a resolution of independence, and approves the Declaration two days later. Congress then begins debating the plan of confederation prepared by a committee chaired by John Dickinson. But in August it postpones further action and turns its attention to the war, which goes badly for the Americans until George Washington captures a Hessian garrison at Trenton, New Jersey, on Christmas Day.

1777 British troops under General William Howe occupy Philadelphia, the American capital; but in October a second enemy army, commanded by General John Burgoyne, surrenders at Saratoga, New York. Congress then completes the Articles of Confederation and asks the states to ratify this first federal constitution promptly.

1778 In February, in response to the military news from America, France signs treaties of alliance and commerce with the United States. Britain sends a peace commission to America, offering concessions that the colonists would have accepted two years earlier, but which they reject now. In June, American forces under Washington fight an indecisive battle at Monmouth, New Jersey, as the British abandon Philadelphia to concentrate their forces around New York City.

1779   As a prolonged *sitzkrieg* begins in the North, the British shift active military operations to Georgia and South Carolina.

1780   Massachusetts becomes the first state to adopt its constitution by summoning a special constitutional convention for that purpose, then by submitting the proposed constitution for ratification by the people, gathered in their town meetings. New York becomes the first state to cede its claims on interior western lands to the Union.

1781   Maryland, the last holdout state, ratifies the Articles of Confederation, which finally take effect on March 1. Congress has already sent to the states its first proposed amendment, requesting authority to collect an impost on foreign imports. In September, at Yorktown, a joint Franco-American force besieges the main British army operating in the South under the command of Lord Cornwallis. The British surrender on October 18.

1782   In February, the House of Commons votes for an end to the American war. Rhode Island rejects the impost. On November 30, in Paris, John Adams, Benjamin Franklin, John Jay, and Henry Laurens sign a preliminary peace treaty with British envoys.

1783   After months of debate and amid rumors of unrest in the
                Continental Army, Congress submits a new package of
                revenue-related amendments to the states.

1784   In response to discriminatory British commercial mea-
                sures, Congress proposes two further amendments seek-
                ing limited authority to regulate foreign trade. Accepting
                Virginia's cession of its western land claims gives Congress
                jurisdiction over the Northwest Territory. Thomas Jeffer-
                son privately publishes *Notes on the State of Virginia,* while
                serving as an American diplomat in France.

1785   After meeting successively in Philadelphia, Princeton,
                Annapolis, and Trenton since 1783, Congress settles in
                New York City and makes it the nation's capital.

1786   Virginia adopts the Statute for Religious Freedom which
                Jefferson drafted in 1777, effectively disestablishing the
                Episcopal Church. At Virginia's invitation, eight states ap-
                point commissioners to meet in Annapolis to consider
                how best to vest Congress with general authority over
                commerce. Only twelve delegates from five states appear
                in September, among them James Madison, Alexander
                Hamilton, and John Dickinson. Rather than adjourn
                without doing anything, they propose a second general
                conference to meet in Philadelphia in May 1787. Virginia
                again invites the other states to attend, and appoints a

1786   distinguished delegation that includes George Washing-
              ton, George Mason (the leading author of Virginia's own
              constitution of 1776), and James Madison.

1787   In February, Congress endorses the coming convention.
              By April, every state except Rhode Island has agreed to
              attend and has appointed delegates. Madison returns to
              Congress and begins preparing a working agenda for the
              convention. When a quorum of states fails to appear on
              May 14, the appointed day, the Virginia delegation begins
              caucusing and then drafts the Virginia Plan, based sub-
              stantially on Madison's ideas. The convention first for-
              mally meets, eleven days late, on May 25, and elects Wash-
              ington as its presiding officer. Serious deliberation begins
              after Governor Edmund Randolph presents the Virginia
              Plan on May 29. On June 14, William Paterson introduces
              an alternative New Jersey Plan, which would modestly
              modify the Articles of Confederation. After the New Jer-
              sey Plan is briefly discussed and rejected, debate focuses
              on the rules of representation in the new bicameral legis-
              lature the Virginia Plan proposes to create. In early July,
              the convention agrees to apportion representation in the
              lower house on the basis of population, with slaves
              counted as three-fifths of free persons. On July 16, the
              convention narrowly agrees to allow the states to be rep-
              resented equally in the upper house. From July 26 to Au-
              gust 5, a committee of detail converts the resolutions ad-
              opted so far into a working text of a constitution. After

the delegates reconvene on August 6, debate focuses on the legislative powers of Congress and the design of the presidency. Critical decisions on the executive are made on September 4–8. The Constitution is then sent to a committee of style, led by Gouverneur Morris, which re-shapes the resolutions into the seven articles of the final draft. On September 17, thirty-nine of the forty-two delegates still attending sign the completed Constitution. Ratification is debated as the Continental Congress agrees to submit the Constitution to the states; the state legislatures begin scheduling elections to the ratification conventions, whose consent is required. In October, Hamilton, John Jay, and Madison begin publishing their *Federalist* essays in support of ratification.

1788   By early January, five states have ratified the Constitution. In February, Massachusetts becomes the first state to propose amendments while ratifying. On June 21, New Hampshire provides the ninth vote necessary for the Constitution to take effect. A sharply divided Virginia convention ratifies four days later; and a similarly divided New York convention, a month after that. Rhode Island and North Carolina initially reject the Constitution.

1789   Federalist supporters of the Constitution dominate the first elections for the new government. On June 8, Madison introduces proposed amendments to the Constitution in the House of Representatives. In September, Con-

1789   gress sends twelve amendments to the states. North Caro-
        lina ratifies the Constitution in November. Thomas Jef-
        ferson, recently returned from France, accepts appoint-
        ment as the first secretary of state.

1790   Rhode Island ratifies and rejoins the Union, which has
        barely noticed its absence. Treasury Secretary Alexander
        Hamilton presents his first Report on Public Credit, argu-
        ably the greatest state paper in American history.

1791   Over constitutional objections from Madison, Congress
        approves a charter of incorporation for the Bank of the
        United States as recommended by Hamilton. Jefferson
        and Madison urge Washington to veto the bank bill on
        constitutional grounds, but the president accepts
        Hamilton's argument that the Necessary and Proper
        Clause provides adequate authority. In December, the
        Virginia legislature provides the final vote needed to rat-
        ify ten of the twelve amendments proposed by Congress
        in 1789.

1793   After Washington unilaterally declares a policy of Ameri-
        can neutrality in the war between revolutionary France
        and its reactionary enemies, Hamilton and Madison (writ-
        ing, respectively, as "Pacificus" and "Helvidius") dispute
        the source and extent of presidential authority in foreign
        relations. Their essays frame a debate that continues more
        than two centuries later.

1795   The Senate secretly ratifies a controversial treaty negoti-
              ated by Chief Justice John Jay with Britain, resolving out-
              standing issues from the peace treaty of 1783 and new dis-
              putes stemming from British seizure of hundreds of
              American merchantmen in 1793. The Eleventh Amend-
              ment is ratified.

1796   Opposition Republican party critics unsuccessfully at-
              tempt to block implementation of the Jay Treaty by argu-
              ing that the appropriation power of the House of Repre-
              sentatives allows it to withhold funding even after
              ratification by the Senate makes the treaty part of the "su-
              preme law of the land." In *Hylton v. United States,* the Su-
              preme Court decides that a federal tax on carriages is not
              a "direct tax" requiring apportionment among the states
              on the basis of population. This is the first occasion on
              which the Court subjects an act of Congress to constitu-
              tional review. After President Washington announces his
              retirement, the first contested presidential election ends
              with Federalist Vice President John Adams edging out Jef-
              ferson by three electoral votes.

1798   During the Quasi-War with France (also known as the
              Franco-American War), a Federalist-dominated Congress
              and President John Adams adopt the Alien and Sedition
              Acts to repress domestic political opposition. Madison
              and Vice President Jefferson, respectively, draft the Vir-
              ginia and Kentucky Resolutions, arguing that the states,

1798	as original parties to the Union, have authority to protest and perhaps even thwart implementation of constitutionally doubtful acts of the national government.
1800	Republican Party candidates Jefferson and Aaron Burr each receive seventy-three electoral votes, throwing the presidential election into a lame-duck House of Representatives, where the losing Federalist Party can determine the outcome.
1801	The outgoing Federalist Congress enacts the Judiciary Act, expanding the size of the federal judiciary to accommodate "midnight appointments" of members of their party, including new Chief Justice John Marshall. After thirty-six ballots, the House of Representatives elects Jefferson president.
1802	Congress repeals the Judiciary Act of 1801, abolishing many of the new judgeships the earlier act created.
1803	The Supreme Court hears and decides *Marbury v. Madison,* the case in which Chief Justice Marshall is often (though wrongly) said to have "established" the principle of judicial review. A week after deciding *Marbury,* the Court, in *Stuart v. Laird,* upholds the repeal of the Judiciary Act of 1801, thereby ducking a direct confrontation with the Republican-dominated Congress. The Louisiana

Purchase adds vast trans-Mississippi tracts to the territory of the United States.

1804   The Twelfth Amendment is ratified, altering procedures for presidential elections by requiring electors to cast separate votes for president and vice president.

1805   Justice Samuel Chase is impeached for alleged misconduct in the Sedition Act trials, but the Senate fails to convict.

1808   Congress exercises its authority under the Commerce Clause to end American participation in the international slave trade, and, more controversially, to impose an embargo on the sailing of American merchant ships in response to the violations of neutral rights by the warring powers of France and Britain.

1812   Congress declares war on Britain over violations of American claims of neutral rights.

1815   The Hartford Convention of New England Federalists opposed to the War of 1812 proposes an array of constitutional amendments. All are ignored during jubilation over the Treaty of Ghent, which ended the war, and the American victory at New Orleans.

1819   In *McCulloch v. Maryland,* the Supreme Court upholds the constitutionality of the federally chartered Second Bank of the United States, relying on the same arguments Hamilton laid down in 1791. In *Dartmouth v. Woodward,* the Court treats provisions of a state charter as equivalent to a contract, in order to overturn a modification of the charter of Dartmouth College by the New Hampshire legislature. Virginia jurists, led by Spencer Roane, argue that judgments of the Supreme Court cannot be binding on the states.

1820   The Missouri Compromise resolves congressional controversy over admission of Missouri to the Union as a slave state, in part by barring the spread of slavery into the territory acquired through the Louisiana Purchase north of the 36′30″ parallel.

1824   In *Gibbons v. Ogden,* the Supreme Court offers an expansive interpretation of the authority of Congress under the Commerce Clause.

1825   The presidential election again goes into the House of Representatives, after none of the five Republican candidates receives a majority of electoral votes. Ignoring the popular plurality for Andrew Jackson, the House elects John Quincy Adams, son of the second president, John Adams.

1826   By an act of nature or nature's god, Thomas Jefferson and John Adams, good friends, estranged political rivals, and amiable correspondents in retirement, both die on the fiftieth anniversary of the Declaration of Independence.

1830   Senators Daniel Webster (New Hampshire) and Robert Hayne (South Carolina) engage in a major debate over the location of sovereignty in the American federal system. Webster defends a nationalist conception based on "We the People"; Hayne argues a states'-rights view predicated on the irreducible sovereignty of the states as compacting parties to the Constitution.

1832   Escalating South Carolina protests against the modestly protectionist "Tariff of Abominations" of 1828 lead to the calling of a special convention which adopts an ordinance of nullification, declaring the tariff of no effect within the state's borders. In *Worcester v. Georgia,* the Supreme Court wrestles with the problem of defining the legal and constitutional status of Indian nations.

1833   Congress adopts the Force Act threatening enforcement of federal law in South Carolina, while also lowering the protested tariffs, allowing both national and state governments to claim victory in their struggle. In *Barron v. Baltimore,* the Supreme Court holds that the rights enumerated in the first eight amendments to the Constitution apply only against the national government, not the states.

1835   After thirty-four years as chief justice, John Marshall dies on July 6, to be succeeded by Roger Taney of Maryland, who serves until his death in 1864.

1836   Both houses of Congress develop "gag rules" to respond to a flood of antislavery petitions. Former president John Quincy Adams, now a member of the House, launches a running campaign to overturn and circumvent this restriction on the people's First Amendment right to petition. On June 28, the last surviving framer of the Constitution, James Madison, dies at his Montpelier estate near Orange, Virginia.

1837   In the *Charles River Bridge* case, the Supreme Court permits Massachusetts to revoke a monopolistic contract granted to one company.

1842   In *Prigg v. Pennsylvania,* the Supreme Court upholds the Fugitive Slave Act of 1793, but leaves the states free to avoid assisting in its enforcement. Congress requires all members of the House of Representatives to be elected in districts, barring states from choosing their representatives statewide.

1845   The bankrupt independent republic of Texas is annexed to the Union by a joint resolution of Congress, rather than by the treaty originally proposed. That would have required a two-thirds vote of the Senate, which might have been unobtainable because acquisition of Texas would greatly expand the territory open to slavery.

1846   Congress declares war on Mexico, which has refused to recognize the Texas annexation. The House debates the Wilmot Proviso, which would bar the spread of slavery into any territories acquired from Mexico.

1848   By the treaty of Guadalupe Hidalgo, the United States acquires territory covering the future states of Arizona, New Mexico, and California, as well as parts of Colorado, Utah, and Nevada, from Mexico.

1850   In the last great intersectional compromise, Congress provides for the admission of California as a free state, abolishes the slave trade in Washington, D.C., and passes a harsh Fugitive Slave Act to placate slaveholders.

1854   The Kansas-Nebraska Act replaces the Missouri Compromise prohibition on slavery north of 36′30″ with a doctrine of "popular sovereignty" enabling settlers to determine whether their territories would be open to slavery.

1857   In *Dred Scott v. Sandford,* a splintered Supreme Court rejects claims by appellant Scott that previous residence in Illinois and the Minnesota territory made him a free man, and that he could not be held as a slave after his return to Missouri. In his plurality opinion, Chief Justice Taney de-

1857   clares that the adopters of the Constitution never imagined that African Americans, even if free, could acquire
the rights of citizens. He also holds that the Missouri
Compromise unconstitutionally deprived slaveholders
of their right to take their human property into the territories.

1858   In a series of debates, Illinois Senator Stephen A. Douglas
and his Republican challenger, Abraham Lincoln, discuss
the slavery question.

1860   Lincoln captures the presidency with electoral votes
drawn solely from northern states. Alarmed southern
states actively begin contemplating secession as they fear
permanent loss of control over the political branches of
the national government.

1861   Reacting to Lincoln's election, seven southern states se-
cede by February 1 and organize a new government of the
Confederate States of America. The lame-duck Thirty-
Sixth Congress entertains an array of constitutional
amendments to resolve the sectional controversy. Lincoln's refusal to surrender Fort Sumter in Charleston Harbor leads to outbreak of the Civil War, and four additional
states join the Confederacy. Lincoln begins mobilizing the
federal government to put down the rebellion before calling the Thirty-Seventh Congress into special session on
July 4. Numerous slaves, sometimes known euphemisti -

cally as "contrabands," begin seeking freedom behind Union lines whenever it becomes physically possible to do so. Congress passes the first Confiscation Act, permitting their emancipation.

1862   Lincoln signs the Emancipation Proclamation on September 22, freeing slaves held behind Confederate lines. The Proclamation is to take effect with the new year. Congress adopts additional acts to undo slavery, including its outright abolition in the District of Columbia.

1863   Congress adopts the Habeas Corpus Act, two years after Lincoln first suspended the Great Writ by executive action. Following the Union victory at Gettysburg, Pennsylvania, Lincoln delivers the Gettysburg Address, linking his vision of constitutional nationhood with the promise of human equality set forth in the Declaration of Independence.

1865   Ratification of the Thirteenth Amendment, abolishing slavery. The collapse of Confederate military resistance and the end of hostilities are followed by the assassination of Lincoln at Ford's Theater in Washington on April 14. Vice President Andrew Johnson, a pro-Unionist Democrat from Tennessee, succeeds to the presidency. His excessively moderate policy toward the defeated and occupied Confederacy and his toleration of the Black Codes with which its provisional governments sought to yoke

1865   the meaning of emancipation lead the Thirty-Ninth Congress that convenes late in the year to consider a more thorough reconstruction of the South. In December, Congress appoints a Joint Committee on Reconstruction, which frames legal and constitutional reforms designed to provide civil rights to freedmen and protect Republican supporters throughout the South. Congress balks at seating the delegations that the former states of the Confederacy send to Washington.

1866   In response to reports of discriminatory and violent acts perpetrated on freedmen, Congress enacts a landmark Civil Rights Act over the veto of President Johnson. To resolve doubts about the act's constitutionality, it also proposes the Fourteenth Amendment. Section 1 of that amendment redefines the nature of American citizenship and lays down three jurisprudential principles that prohibit public authorities in the states from violating the rights of citizens.

1867   Congress adopts the first Military Reconstruction Act, to provide a legal basis for the regular use of federal troops in maintaining law and order throughout the occupied South and in supporting the new governments being elected with significant African American participation, both at the polls and in officeholding. To return delegations to Congress, former Confederate states are required to ratify the Fourteenth Amendment.

1868   President Johnson is impeached, ostensibly for attempt-
        ing to fire Secretary of War Edwin Stanton, whose posi-
        tion Congress tried to place beyond presidential removal
        by the Tenure of Office Act of 1867, a law of doubtful con-
        stitutionality. Johnson escapes conviction and removal by
        a single vote.

1870   Ratification of the Fifteenth Amendment, prohibiting
        race or previous enslavement from being used to justify
        denial of suffrage.

1873   In the *Slaughterhouse Cases,* a divided Supreme Court first
        interprets Section 1 of the Fourteenth Amendment.

1875   Congress adopts its last great Reconstruction measure,
        the Civil Rights Act of 1875, which blocks additional
        forms of racial discrimination emerging in the South by
        promoting free access to public accommodations, com-
        mon carriers, and other facilities.

1877   The presidential election of 1876 produces a confused re-
        sult, with the Republican Rutherford Hayes receiving a
        minority of the national popular vote, while his Demo-
        cratic opponent, Samuel Tilden, appears to be one vote
        short of an electoral majority, with the results from three
        southern states plus Oregon in dispute. After a bipartisan
        electoral commission with a Republican majority resolves
        these disputes in favor of Hayes, continued Democratic

1877   protests of foul play lead to an agreement effectively end-
        ing Reconstruction through the withdrawal of Union
        troops from the South.

1878   In *Reynolds v. United States,* the Supreme Court upholds
        legislation banning the Mormon practice of polygamy in
        the Utah Territory. The Court's interpretation of the Free-
        Exercise Clause of the First Amendment invokes the same
        distinction between protected belief and behavior subject
        to regulation that John Locke drew two centuries earlier
        in his *Letter Concerning Toleration.*

1883   In the *Civil Rights Cases,* the Supreme Court guts the Civil
        Rights Act of 1875 by holding that the discriminatory acts
        denying African Americans access to various public ac-
        commodations and common carriers were constitu-
        tional.

1895   In *Pollock v. United States* the Supreme Court strikes down
        a federal income tax, on the problematic grounds that it is
        a direct tax requiring apportionment among the states on
        the basis of population.

1896   In *Plessy v. Ferguson,* the Supreme Court gives further le-
        gitimacy to the developing practices of racial segregation.
        Under the "separate but equal" doctrine, legal segregation
        of the races is deemed not to violate the norm of equal

protection if the arrangements provided for whites and blacks are substantially equal in quality.

1901   In the *Insular Cases,* the Supreme Court considers how constitutional norms apply to overseas territories acquired by conquest in the Spanish American War of 1898.

1905   In *Lochner v. New York,* the Supreme Court overturns a statute limiting the working hours of bakers as an improper exercise of the state's "police powers" to legislate broadly on behalf of public health, safety, and welfare. This decision is commonly linked to the doctrine of substantive due process.

1908   In *Muller v. Oregon,* the Supreme Court upholds a statute limiting the working hours of women, arguing that gender creates a legitimate rationale for public regulation.

1913   Ratification of the Sixteenth Amendment, providing for a federal income tax, and the Seventeenth Amendment, providing for the popular election of senators.

1917   Following the Germans' announcement of a campaign of unlimited submarine warfare against merchant shipping, Congress declares war on Germany.

1919   Ratification of the Nineteenth Amendment, commonly known as Prohibition. In *Schenck v. United States* and espe-

1919	cially *Abrams v. United States,* Justice Oliver Wendell Holmes begins to develop the stricter "clear and present danger" test for public regulation of political speech, which previously was subject to the "bad tendency" standard that permitted officials to prosecute dissenters more easily. The Senate rejects the Treaty of Versailles, negotiated by President Woodrow Wilson.
1920	Ratification of the Nineteenth Amendment, which enfranchises women, culminating decades of suffragist activity.
1923	In *Adkins v. Children's Hospital,* the Supreme Court strikes down a congressional statute setting a minimum wage for women and children working in the nation's capital. The reasoning of the case is applicable to similar laws in numerous other states, and symbolizes the extent to which the Court opposed broad public regulation of economic activity.
1933	Franklin D. Roosevelt is elected president with solidly Democratic majorities in Congress. His "hundred days" of New Deal legislation are a response to the Great Depression, triggered by the stock market collapse of October 1929. Ratification of the Twentieth Amendment, advancing dates when a new Congress first meets and presidents are inaugurated. Ratification by state conventions of the Twenty-First Amendment, repealing Prohibition.

A CALENDAR OF EVENTS

1935   In *Schechter Poultry v. United States,* the Supreme Court
            overturns key provisions of the National Industrial Re-
            covery Act of 1933 as an improper application of the Com-
            merce Clause and an improper delegation of authority to
            the executive. Subsequent decisions voiding other New
            Deal acts produce mounting political criticism of the
            Court as a reactionary institution.

1936   Roosevelt's reelection sets the stage for escalating con-
            frontation with the Court. In *United States v. Curtiss-
            Wright Export Corp.,* Justice George Sutherland lays down
            a problematic theory of the extent of executive power
            over foreign relations.

1937   In February, Roosevelt announces his "court-packing"
            plan to expand the membership of the Supreme Court as
            sitting justices reach the age of seventy. With Justice
            Owen Roberts shifting his position on key issues, the
            Court reverses course and begins accepting both New
            Deal and state regulatory actions it previously invalidated.

1940   Roosevelt shatters the two-term presidential precedent
            set by George Washington in 1796.

1941   Taking advantage of his powers as commander-in-chief of
            the armed forces, Roosevelt orders U.S. naval forces to
            protect transatlantic convoys bringing aid to Great Brit-
            ain. Japan attacks the American fleet at Pearl Harbor,

1941   Hawai'i, and its ally, Germany, then declares war on the United States, making the nation a full participant in the Second World War.

1942   Over weak opposition from the Department of Justice and with strong support from the Department of War, Roosevelt issues Executive Order 9066, providing for the internment of tens of thousands of Japanese American citizens in western states in a blatant denial of due process and other fundamental rights. In *Hirabayashi v. United States* (1943), the Supreme Court upholds the internment policy, but in the subsequent case of *Korematsu v. United States* (1944), passionate dissenting opinions evince growing discomfort with the Court's passive acquiescence and a renewed interest in reviving the Equal-Protection Clause of the Fourteenth Amendment on behalf of racial minorities.

1944   In *Smith v. Allwright,* the Supreme Court prohibits the Democratic Party of Texas from limiting voting in primary elections to whites only, citing the involvement of the state in conducting elections.

1948   In *Shelley v. Kraemer,* the Supreme Court overturns a previous ruling of 1926 and prohibits the enforcement of covenants restricting the sale of housing on racial grounds.

1950   Without seeking a declaration of war from Congress, President Truman orders the armed forces to oppose the North Korean invasion of South Korea.

1951   Ratification of the Twenty-Second Amendment, limiting presidents to two elected terms in office.

1952   In *Youngstown Sheet and Tube Company v. Sawyer,* the Supreme Court rules 6-to-3 against President Truman's seizure of the steel mills, ostensibly justified by the need to maintain production during the Korean War while steelworkers strike. The concurring opinion of Justice Robert Jackson later comes to be recognized as a virtual doctrine by which courts can judge assertions of executive authority over matters of national security. In December, the Court hears oral argument in the consolidated cases known as *Brown v. Board of Education,* which challenge the racial segregation of primary and secondary schools. It then asks for reargument on the original meaning of the Fourteenth Amendment.

1953   The newly elected president, Dwight D. Eisenhower, appoints Governor Earl Warren of California as chief justice, replacing Chief Justice Vinson, who died suddenly. The *Brown* reargument occurs in December.

1954   On May 17 the Court hands down its landmark ruling in *Brown,* holding that racially segregated education is inher-

| 1954 | ently unequal because of the psychological stigma it attaches to the group against whom segregation is directed. The "separate but equal" doctrine associated with *Plessy v. Ferguson* is repudiated, though not explicitly mentioned in the opinion. The Court asks for further argument on the remedies to be applied. |

| 1955 | In *Brown II,* the Court rules that lower courts hearing desegregation suits must use "all deliberate speed" in devising remedies. In Montgomery, Alabama, a boycott of the city bus system led by the young minister Martin Luther King Jr. illustrates the mounting opposition of African Americans to other Jim Crow practices of racial segregation. |

| 1961 | Ratification of the Twenty-Third Amendment, granting the District of Columbia electoral votes. |

| 1962 | In *Baker v. Carr* and the later case of *Reynolds v. Sims* (1964), the Supreme Court initiates the reapportionment revolution that soon requires state legislators and congressional representatives to be elected in districts of equal population, according to the principle of one person, one vote. |

| 1963 | In *Gideon v. Wainwright,* the Supreme Court affirms that indigent defendants accused of crimes in state proceed- |

ings must be granted their Sixth Amendment right to counsel. This is one of numerous rulings relating to the criminal justice system that make the heyday of the Warren Court one of the most celebrated and criticized epochs in American jurisprudential history. President John F. Kennedy is assinated in Dallas on November 22.

1964   Responding to popular protests against racial segregation and discrimination, Congress adopts a new Civil Rights Act with eleven separate titles affecting various activities. The most significant is Title VII, relating to employment practices. In August, Congress passes the Tonkin Gulf Resolution, giving President Lyndon B. Johnson effective authority to escalate the American military commitment to the anti-Communist regime in South Vietnam. Ratification of Twenty-Fourth Amendment, abolishing poll taxes.

1965   Following the Freedom Summer of 1964, when college students attempted to register African American voters in the South, Congress approves the Voting Rights Act, which launches a Second Reconstruction. In *Griswold v. Connecticut,* a case involving the access of married couples to contraception, the Supreme Court recognizes a general right to privacy, located not in any specific provision of the Constitution but in "penumbras, formed by emanations" from the Bill of Rights generally.

1967   President Johnson nominates Thurgood Marshall to the Supreme Court. Long the driving force behind the National Association for the Advancement of Colored People's legal campaign against segregation, Marshall becomes the first African American to sit on the Court. Ratification of the Twenty-Fifth Amendment, principally concerned with presidential succession and disability.

1969   President Richard Nixon nominates Warren Burger to replace retiring Chief Justice Earl Warren.

1971   Ratification of the Twenty-Sixth Amendment, lowering the voting age to eighteen.

1972   On the evening of June 17, five burglars are arrested in a mysterious break-in at the Democratic National Committee offices in the Watergate complex in Washington, D.C. The perpetrators are soon discovered to have links to officials in the Nixon administration.

1973   In an effort to constrain unilateral presidential warmaking, Congress adopts the War Powers Act over a veto by President Nixon. In *Roe v. Wade,* the Supreme Court recognizes a woman's decision to have an abortion as a fundamental right. The conspiracy to cover up the origins and circumstances of the Watergate burglary of 1972 begins to unravel as a Senate Select Committee interviews officials, and leaks to the *Washington Post* expose key details of the ongoing criminal investigations.

1974   In *United States v. Nixon,* the Supreme Court rejects a presidential effort to quash a subpoena seeking White House tapes of confidential conversations in the Oval Office—discussions relevant to the prosecution of administration officials indicted for obstruction of justice in the Watergate proceedings. Once released, the tapes expose President Nixon's complicity in the obstruction of justice. In August, the House Judiciary Committee votes two articles of impeachment against him. With his political support collapsing, the president resigns his office.

1983   President Ronald Reagan nominates Stanford Law School graduate Sandra Day O'Connor to be the first female justice on the Supreme Court.

1984   A public speech by Attorney Edwin Meese, calling for a return to a "jurisprudence of original interpretation," triggers ongoing public and academic controversy over the theory of "originalism," which holds that constitutional interpretation should be faithful to the original meaning of the text, or the original intentions of its ratifiers, or some combination thereof, to be determined by jurisprudential alchemy.

1992   Ratification of the Twenty-Seventh Amendment, affect-
            ing congressional pay raises, a mere two centuries after it
            was originally proposed.

1998   After being deposed in a civil lawsuit concerning his al-
            leged harassment of a state employee during his tenure as
            governor of Arkansas, President Bill Clinton is accused of
            lying about a sexual relationship with a White House in-
            tern. In December, the House of Representatives ap-
            proves two impeachment charges against him, one for
            perjury before a grand jury, the other for obstruction of
            justice.

1999   Following a trial of five weeks, the Senate acquits Clinton.

2000   In the presidential election, the Democratic candidate, Al
            Gore, carries the national popular vote against George W.
            Bush, but the outcome in the electoral college pivots on
            the results in Florida, where Bush leads by only hundreds
            of votes. The nation is transfixed as recounts proceed in
            selected counties requested by Gore, and as litigation
            over the procedures to be used bounces back and forth
            between state and federal courts. In *Bush v. Gore,* the Su-
            preme Court finally intervenes to halt the recount, with a
            bloc of five conservative justices, all Republican appoin-
            tees, rallying around two distinct theories as to why the
            recount cannot be completed.

2003   Five outs away from playing in their first World Series since the end of World War II, the Chicago Cubs blow a 3-to-0 lead in the eighth inning of game 6 when a spectator interferes with a catchable foul ball, then lose game 7 to the Florida Marlins. Yet hope springs eternal in the human breast.

2006   In *Hamdan v. Rumsfeld,* the Supreme Court holds (5 to 3, with recently appointed Chief Justice John Roberts recused) that the Bush administration lacks unilateral authority under the Uniform Code of Military Justice to establish military commissions to try the "enemy combatants" held at Guantánamo Bay, Cuba, following the terrorist attacks of September 11, 2001, and the ensuing American military operations in Afghanistan. The decision is widely regarded as a decisive rebuke to the administration's extraordinarily broad claims for executive power in wartime.

2008   In *District of Columbia v. Heller,* the Supreme Court discovers that the Second Amendment protects an individual right to keep firearms. In *Boumediene v. George W. Bush,* it holds that federal courts may entertain *habeas corpus* pleas from enemy combatants detained in the "war on terror."

Further Reading

The literature is vast; the topics, numerous; the controversies, endless; the value, priceless—because this is how Americans have defined themselves as a people.

Ackerman, Bruce. *The Failure of the Founding Fathers: Jefferson, Marshall, and the Rise of Presidential Democracy.* Cambridge, Mass.: Harvard University Press, 2005.

Amar, Akhil Reed. *America's Constitution: A Biography.* New York: Random House, 2005.

Armitage, David. *The Declaration of Independence: A Global History.* Cambridge, Mass.: Harvard University Press, 2007.

Bailyn, Bernard. *The Ideological Origins of the American Revolution.* Enlarged ed. Cambridge, Mass.: Harvard University Press, 1992.

——, ed. *The Debate on the Constitution.* 2 vols. New York: Library of America, 1993.

Beard, Charles A. *An Economic Interpretation of the Constitution of the United States.* New York: Macmillan, 1913.

Becker, Carl L. *The Declaration of Independence: A Study in the History of Political Ideas.* New York: Knopf, 1942 (1922).

Beeman, Richard. *Plain, Honest Men: The Making of the American Constitution.* New York: Random House, 2009.

Beer, Samuel H. *To Make a Nation: The Rediscovery of American Federalism.* Cambridge, Mass.: Harvard University Press, 1993.

Berkin, Carol. *A Brilliant Solution: Inventing the American Constitution.* New York: Harcourt, 2002.

Bernstein, Richard. *Are We to Be a Nation? The Making of the Constitution.* Cambridge, Mass.: Harvard University Press, 1987.

Bickel, Alexander C. *The Least Dangerous Branch: The Supreme Court at the Bar of Politics.* Indianapolis: Bobbs-Merrill, 1962.

Bogus, Carl, ed. *The Second Amendment in Law and History.* New York: New Press, 2000.

Curtis, Michael Kent. *No State Shall Abridge: The 14th Amendment and the Bill of Rights.* Durham, N.C.: Duke University Press, 1986.

DuBois, Ellen Carol. *Woman Suffrage and Women's Rights.* New York: New York University Press, 1998.

Ellis, Richard E. *Aggressive Nationalism: McCulloch v. Maryland and the Foundation of Federal Authority in the Young Republic.* New York: Oxford University Press, 2007.

Farber, Daniel. *Lincoln's Constitution.* Chicago: University of Chicago Press, 2003.

Fehrenbacher, Don. *The Dred Scott Case: Its Significance in American Law and Politics.* New York: Oxford University Press, 1978.

Fliegelman, Jay. *Declaring Independence: Jefferson, Natural Language, and the Culture of Performance.* Stanford, Calif.: Stanford University Press, 1993.

Garraty, John A., ed. *Quarrels That Have Shaped the Constitution.* Rev. ed. New York: Harper and Row, 1987.

Gillman, Howard. *The Constitution Besieged: The Rise and Demise of*

Lochner Era Police Powers Jurisprudence. Durham, N.C.: Duke University Press, 1993.

Goldwin, Robert A. *From Parchment to Power: How James Madison Used the Bill of Rights to Save the Constitution.* Washington, D.C.: AEI Press, 1997.

Gordon, Sarah Barringer. *The Mormon Question: Polygamy and Constitutional Conflict in Nineteenth-Century America.* Chapel Hill: University of North Carolina Press, 2002.

Hyman, Harold, and William M. Wiecek. *Equal Justice under Law: Constitutional Development, 1835–1875.* New York: Harper and Row, 1982.

Kammen, Michael G. *A Machine That Would Go of Itself: The Constitution in American Culture.* New York: Knopf, 1986.

Kerber, Linda. *No Constitutional Right to Be Ladies: Women and the Rights of Citizenship.* New York: Hill and Wang, 1998.

Kettner, James H. *The Development of American Citizenship, 1608–1870.* Chapel Hill: University of North Carolina Press, 1978.

Keyssar, Alexander. *The Right to Vote: The Contested History of Democracy in America.* New York: Basic Books, 2000.

Killenbeck, Mark. *M'Culloch v. Maryland: Securing a Nation.* Lawrence: University Press of Kansas, 2006.

Klarman, Michael J. *From Jim Crow to Civil Rights: The Supreme Court and the Struggle for Racial Equality.* New York: Oxford University Press, 2004.

Kramer, Larry D. *The People Themselves: Popular Constitutionalism and Judicial Review.* New York: Oxford University Press, 2004.

Kutler, Stanley. *Privilege and Creative Destruction: The Charles River Bridge Case.* Philadelphia: Lippincott, 1971.

Kyvig, David. *Explicit and Authentic Acts: Amending the U.S. Constitution, 1789–1995.* Lawrence: University Press of Kansas, 1985.

Leuchtenberg, William E. *The Supreme Court Reborn: The Constitutional Revolution in the Age of Roosevelt*. New York: Oxford University Press, 1995.

Levinson, Sanford. *Our Undemocratic Constitution: Where the Constitution Goes Wrong (and How We the People Can Correct It)*. New York: Oxford University Press, 2006.

Levy, Leonard. *Original Intent and the Framers' Constitution*. New York: Macmillan, 1988.

Lewis, Anthony. *Gideon's Trumpet*. New York: Random House, 1964.

Lofgren, Charles A. *The Plessy Case: A Legal-Historical Interpretation*. New York: Oxford University Press, 1987.

Maier, Pauline. *American Scripture: Making the Declaration of Independence*. New York: Knopf, 1997.

Marcus, Maeva. *Truman and the Steel Seizure Case: The Limits of Presidential Power*. New York: Columbia University Press, 1977.

McCloskey, Robert. *The American Supreme Court*. 4th rev. ed. Chicago: University of Chicago Press, 2005.

McDonald, Forrest. *Novus Ordo Seclorum: The Intellectual Origins of the Constitution*. Lawrence: University Press of Kansas, 1985.

Neely, Mark E. *The Fate of Liberty: Abraham Lincoln and Civil Liberties*. New York: Oxford University Press, 1991.

Nelson, William E. *The Fourteenth Amendment: From Political Principle to Judicial Doctrine*. Cambridge, Mass.: Harvard University Press, 1988.

Newmyer, R. Kent. *John Marshall and the Heroic Age of the Supreme Court*. Baton Rouge: Louisiana State University Press, 2001.

Patterson, James T. *Brown v. Board of Education: A Civil Rights Milestone and Its Troubled Legacy*. New York: Oxford University Press, 2001.

Peters, Shawn Francis. *Judging Jehovah's Witnesses: Religious Persecution and the Dawn of the Rights Revolution.* Lawrence: University Press of Kansas, 2000.

Rakove, Jack N. *Original Meanings: Politics and Ideas in the Making of the Constitution.* New York: Knopf, 1996.

Slauter, Eric. *The State as a Work of Art: The Cultural Origins of the Constitution.* Chicago: University of Chicago Press, 2009.

Stone, Geoffrey. *Perilous Times: Free Speech in Wartime from the Sedition Act of 1798 to the War on Terrorism.* New York: Norton, 2004.

Veit, Helen E., Kenneth R. Bowling, and Charlene Bangs Bickford, eds. *Creating the Bill of Rights: The Documentary Record from the First Federal Congress.* Baltimore: Johns Hopkins University Press, 1991.

Vorenberg, Michael. *Final Freedom: The Civil War, the Abolition of Slavery, and the Thirteenth Amendment.* New York: Cambridge University Press, 2001.

Wood, Gordon S. *The Creation of the American Republic, 1776–1787.* Chapel Hill: University of North Carolina Press, 1969.

Credits

82   National Archives and Records Administration, College Park, Maryland.
83   Photo by Roman Beniaminson. Bildarchiv Preussischer Kulturbesitz / Art Resource, NY.
90   Photo by El Meliani. Réunion des Musées Nationaux / Art Resource, NY.
91   Trumbull Collection, Yale University Art Gallery / Art Resource, NY.
105   National Archives and Records Administration, College Park, Maryland.
137   Photos 12 / Alamy.
139   Photo courtesy of Roscoe Filburn's daughter, Mary Lou (Filbrun [née Filburn]) Spurgeon, and the Trotwood-Madison Historical Society.
141   Classic Image / Alamy.
171   Art Resource, NY.
191   National Archives and Records Administration, College Park, Maryland.
225   National Archives and Records Administration, College Park, Maryland.
237   Copyright © Bettmann/CORBIS.
247   National Archives and Records Administration, College Park, Maryland.
250   National Portrait Gallery, Smithsonian Institution / Art Resource, NY.
257   Photo by Alexander Gardner. Pictoral Press Ltd / Alamy.
261   Art Resource, NY.
263   Copyright © Bettmann/CORBIS.
277   Library of Congress, Prints and Photographs Division, LC-USZ62-123257.

282 Art Resource, NY.

288 AP Photo.

289 National Archive / Getty Images.

298 Library of Congress, LC-USZ62-134844.

303 Photo by Frank Johnston. Copyright © Bettmann/CORBIS.

Acknowledgments

THIRTY-SOME years ago I published my first scholarly essay, "The Decision for American Independence," and for the past quarter-century, thinking about the origins and interpretation of the Constitution has been my main academic preoccupation. In preparing this annotated edition of our two founding documents, I happily confess that I have enjoyed the opportunity of distilling the views I have formed over these decades into the accompanying commentary. Yet I have also been reminded of what an extraordinarily complex and rich subject the story of the American constitutional tradition is, how fortunate I have been to be part of the community of scholars who make it their work, and how much I have learned from the great body of knowledge they have created. Several parts of that community deserve my thanks.

First, and most important, I am deeply grateful to the colleagues who reviewed the introduction and annotations: my friend and neighbor Dean Larry Kramer of the Stanford Law School; Charles McCurdy of the University of Virginia; and Michael Klarman, formerly of Mr. Jefferson's university himself, a graduate of Stanford Law School, and now professor at Harvard Law School. All were helpful in their comments and thorough in their reviews. To Mike Klarman I owe a special measure of devotion for subjecting my musings to the strictest scrutiny imaginable, challenging me to sharpen many points, and saving me from serious miscues. I owe additional thanks to two scholars who share a common interest in one particular clause of the Constitution: Larry Lessig, formerly of Stanford, now at Harvard, too; and Zorina Khan of Bowdoin College.

Then there is that larger group of scholars—historians, political scientists, and legal academics—on whose works I have drawn, with whom I have exchanged views or shared podiums, sometimes argued, and more often, I hope, admired for the contributions they have made. In compiling this next list, I worry about omissions, but in line with the Jeffersonian principle that "half a loaf is better than no bread," it would be remiss of me not to acknowledge as many as I can, in the democratic order of alphabetical recognition: Bruce Ackerman, Akhil Amar, Bernard Bailyn, Carl Bogus, Paul Brest, Gerhard Casper, Saul Cornell, John Ferejohn, Paul Finkelman, Barry Friedman, David Golove, Sally Gordon, Tom Grey, Calvin Johnson, Laura Kalman, John Kaminski, Pam Karlan, Neal Katyal, the late James Kettner, Alex Keyssar, David Konig, David Kyvig, Ralph Lerner, Sandy Levinson, the late Leonard Levy, Charles Lofgren, Ira "Chip" Lupu, Pauline Maier, Bruce Mann, Maeva Marcus, Michael McConnell, Bill Nelson, Peter Onuf, Rick Pildes, Robert Post, Stephen Presser, David Rabban, John Reid, Kathleen Sullivan, Eugene Volokh, Michael Vorenberg, Barry Weingast, and Gordon Wood. This is, again, only a partial list, but in one way or another, in writing or conversation or by email, by example or through criticism, everyone on it has influenced my approach to the great subject of constitutionalism.

I owe a debt as well to the Stanford undergraduates who have taken my various courses on the Revolutionary era and constitutional history, tolerated my numerous digressions, and made me think time and again that I did something right in a past life to be able to spend my teaching career on the Farm. And special recognition to the fabulous constitutional history group from 2001: Emily Cadei, Rachel Scarlett-Trotter Chaney, Anuj Gupta, Joshua David Hawley, Joshua David Hurwit, Caitrin McKiernan, Fiona McNiff, Anitha Reddy, Kim Sandler, and their classmates.

Finally, I am grateful to John Kulka for the invitation to prepare this volume, and to Maria Ascher for the energetic editorial labors necessary to bring it to completion.